LEANING FORWARD!

GENERAL ASSEMBLY

OF THE CHURCH OF GOD IN THE UNITED STATES AND CANADA

Barry L. Callen

EMETH PRESS
www.emethpress.com

Leaning Forward! General Assembly of the Church of God in the United States and Canada.

Library of Congress Cataloging-in-Publication Data

Names: Callen, Barry L., author.
Title: Leaning forward! : General Assembly of the Church of God in the United States and Canada / Barry L. Callen.
Description: Lexington : Emeth Press, Kentucky, 2019. | Includes index. | Summary: "This is the life story of the General Assembly of the Church of God in the United States and Canada. It is rooted in the church realities of the late nineteenth century and now has traveled through many subsequent generations to the present day"-- Provided by publisher.

Identifiers: LCCN 2019039460 (print) | LCCN 2019039461 (ebook) | ISBN 9781609471521 (paperback) | ISBN 9781609471545 (kindle edition)
Subjects: LCSH: Church of God (Anderson, Ind.) General Assembly--History. | Church of God (Anderson, Ind.)--History.
Classification: LCC BX7025 .C35 2019 (print) | LCC BX7025 (ebook) | DDC 289.9--dc23
LC record available at https://lccn.loc.gov/2019039460
LC ebook record available at https://lccn.loc.gov/2019039461

CONTENTS

WHY REMEMBER YESTERDAY?

This is the life story of the General Assembly of the Church of God in the United States and Canada. It's rooted in the harsh church realities of the late nineteenth century and now has traveled through many subsequent generations to the present day.

The church reform movement that this Assembly represents always has sought to "lean forward," reaching in each new time and place for the fullest realization of God's will for individual believers and the church as a whole. That reaching now extends far beyond the circumstances of 1880 and the shores of North America, the limiting boundaries of the movement's humble beginning.

Why remember this Assembly's particular life story? We choose to remember even though we are focused on the new challenges and possibilities of the church in the twenty-first century. We remember because we don't want to proceed blindly. Our sisters and brothers of yesterday have left many markers that we need. We look back with caution, of course. The church has always reflected the limits of its particular times and places. We look back, nonetheless, because we know that God has acted in the past and those actions remain guideposts for our future.

The Church of God movement always has been committed to "going back to the blessed old Bible." Why? Because it believes that this recording of sacred history is a dependable guide to God's future with us. We learn about God and God's ways by reviewing what God did yesterday. God's past tends to point wisely toward God's future. Therefore, in these pages we look back to a few of the church leaders, events, and thinking of yesterday, not to gather the ashes of their campsites but to discover the fire in their souls that should still ignite ours.

The intent of the Church of God always has been for Christian believers to network as a mission-minded "movement," not a fixed institution inflexible and focused on itself. It has been determined to be a living organism of God's gifting, governing, and sending Spirit. There are to be no manipulative ways of group life contrary to New Testament teaching. Central has been awareness that the ongoing quest for personal holiness and the intended result of unity among God's people are necessary to accomplish God's redemptive mission in this world.

From its beginning, the Church of God movement has sought to return to the truths, simplicities, and Spirit-directedness seen in the New Testament and early church. In contrast to binding creeds and domineering church organizations, this movement has attempted to remain open to the fresh and freeing moves of the Spirit of God.

We now honor this movement's beginnings and more than a century of its life as seen in the story of its General Assembly in the United States and Canada. We remember appreciatively and cautiously, resisting the trap of being immobilized by the times, places, and thinking of yesterday. God moves on and God's people must be free to lean forward into that future with fresh insight and obedience. God's future, however, cannot be separated from God's past actions among faithful disciples.

The General Assembly (United States and Canada)

Ministers in the earliest years of the Church of God movement found themselves desiring fellowship, inspiration, and effective avenues of service together. Increasingly, these avenues needed some form of coordination of ministry preparation, planning, and implementation. Informal assemblies of ministers developed and soon came to assume a "business" as well as a strictly "spiritual" nature. By 1917 the most prominent of these assemblies was meeting annually in Anderson, Indiana, where it formalized and became known as the "General Ministerial Assembly." It remained in Anderson for nearly a century.

These pages detail the evolving life, functions, thinking, and actions of this coordinating body now known simply as the "General Assembly." This body is the Church of God movement in the United States and Canada gathered for guiding its life and ministry together. It reflects the movement's best cooperative efforts to be faithful to its sense of divine calling. It embodies a Spirit-centered heritage and also an increasing willingness to "structure" as necessary in order to be good stewards of the common life and mission of the Church of God movement.

This intentional togetherness of the General Assembly has welcomed the diversity of gender, race, and Christian backgrounds, and it has included two nations, the United States and Canada. This diversity has brought great enrichment, and at times the challenge of somewhat differing cultural, political, theological, and legal assumptions. Admittedly, the actions of the General Assembly have come out of the United States setting primarily, but inclusiveness has always been the goal. Diversity is not disunity. Learning how to function well as equal brothers and sisters enriched by diversity is a particular challenge of our time, and it's always been a goal of this movement of the Church of God.

Memory in Service of Tomorrow

The 1951 *Yearbook* of the Church of God carries a "Diamond Jubilee Perspective" that reads: "May we find new vision and conviction to brace us and set us surging forward." Now, after nearly one hundred and forty years after the movement's beginning, the Church of God and its General Assembly in the United States and Canada have so much to look back on with gratitude.

Yes, we look back gratefully, but God's movement must continue surging forward! Thus, this book's title, *Leaning Forward!* While we thank God for yesterday, and dare not lose sight of it, we choose to be focused on today. We are obligated to God for addressing and serving the tomorrow that's soon to arrive.

The history of the General Assembly is organized here in thirty-two brief chapters, grouped by theme in eight sections, with a concluding master Index. This allows the reader easy access to whatever memory is needed to help inform the fresh future now at hand. For instance, the reader will find in these pages important examples of . . .

Organizing Reluctantly. There have been times of organizing reluctantly, first to qualify for clergy railroad discounts (1902), and more recently to face the demands of justice and legal threats to clergy and local churches by authorizing a common *Credentials Manual* (2017). First there was great reluctance to organize and now there is a cautious courage to do what is necessary to lean forward with God. What additional organizing is needed and justified today, not for our own benefit but for the mission of the church?

Avoiding Self-Serving. There have been in the General Assembly both worries about the spiritual risk of approving the starting of a college (1918) and vision for facilitating a gathering of African nations into a more united partnership in service for Christ (2018). How can the Assembly now most effectively oversee and celebrate its four universities and one seminary? What must the General Assembly in North America now do to be a visionary catalyst and not a self-serving colonialist around the world? How can the Assembly on one continent serve those on many?

Moving Beyond Mere Talk. There have been times in the story of the General Assembly when the church has been determined to do something about needed Christian unity instead of just talking about it (see chapter seventeen). How can the Church of God movement today become a leader in and not just a critic of the "ecumenical" movement among Christians worldwide? Can the movement, maybe in part through the General Assembly, finally find its voice and fulfill its role?

Being Convictional But Not Creedal. There have been times of crisis when the General Assembly, while careful not to be creed-setting (see its constitutional limitation in chapter three), has ventured into doctrinal matters. Included have been some addressing of the centrality of Jesus Christ, the revealed authority of the Bible, and biblical guidelines for the receiving and exercising certain divine gifts like "tongues" (see chapters sixteen and twenty-one).

Is it time to share with the wider Body of Christ certain theological perspectives treasured by the Church of God movement and thought needful for all church fellowships? See chapter thirty. Would such sharing be a violation or fulfillment of the reforming heritage of the Church of God movement?

Differing Gracefully Among Ourselves. There have been times of facing the dilemma of resisting church structures yet needing them, wondering how to live well with the ones we have, and treating each other with respect as we grapple with this and many other issues. How can we hear each other's concerns fairly and helpfully? See chapters fourteen and fifteen for past struggles and suggested guidelines. What have been our best conversations and where did they come out? See chapters sixteen, eighteen, twenty-seven, and twenty-eight. Have we struggled together, evolved hard-won wisdom, and then failed to act?

Leaning Forward with God's Guidance. Many of the actions of the General Assembly recalled in chapter twenty-six reflect the church's consistent determination to "lean forward," moving beyond persistent social wrongs so that God's righteous kingdom can be embodied *now*. Realizing Christian unity through common life in God's Spirit is seen in actions of the General Assembly recorded in chapter seventeen. Since the church is one worldwide family of God, this book's final chapters highlight the General Assembly's globe-oriented initiatives. What is God now doing in our troubled world? Is the church willing to question traditional structures, rituals, and attitudes to help make God's will a present reality? Leaning forward with the Spirit is the church's mission.

These are only samples of what follows. They highlight the value that lies in remembering this particular yesterday of the church. We will remember with an eye always on God's intended tomorrow. These chapters are filled with yesterdays that pose questions and prompt fresh possibilities for the church's current life and mission. They deserve our attention and respect, if not our mindless duplication.

The hope is that the values discovered in the history of the General Assembly will be invested in fresh resolve to face the world of today creatively, passionately, and filled with the life God's Spirit. Jesus is the Subject. Reclaiming a lost world is the mission. The General Assembly of the Church of God in the United States and Canada has been and increasingly can be an important tool in the hands of the redeeming God who is the only hope of ourselves and today's world.

Overview

NATURE OF THE ASSEMBLY

The General Assembly of the Church of God movement in the United States and Canada, sometimes referred to here simply as the "Assembly," was formally organized in 1917. It has met regularly ever since as the central feature of the corporate life of the Church of God movement. Today it convenes biennially during the movement's Convention. It has established a legally incorporated non-profit corporation empowered to hold property and act, on the Assembly's behalf and in the pursuit of its ends, when the Assembly is not in session. This corporation is called "Church of God Ministries, Inc." and governed by a Ministries Council accountable to the Assembly.

Key organizational information is found in chapters one through four. Something should be noted, however. The Church of God movement has "organized" only as necessary to function effectively, and only in reference to the work of the church, never the church itself. The primary intent has been to "lean forward," being a flexible movement able to respond as God's Spirit directs.

1

NATURE AND ORGANIZATION

The General Assembly and Church of God Ministries, its corporate body, function in ways intended to fulfill the nature and mission of the Church of God movement in the United States and Canada. Jesus is the Subject and the movement's functioning seeks to be the hands and feet of Jesus all over the world. Historically, the Church of God movement has held important doctrinal distinctives that create a sense of grounding, mission, and interconnectedness among its congregations (see chapter twenty-one).

A prominent feature of the fellowship of the Church of God movement is its unity in diversity. Disciples seek to be one body together, not in spite of but enriched by the diversity of its members and their various giftings by God. There is a prominent and valued presence of racial and gender diversity at all levels of church leadership and ministry. Note in chapter eleven, for instance, that the elected Chair of the General Assembly of the Church of God has been filled capably by leaders of differing races and genders.

There also is national diversity. The General Assembly includes the congregations and pastors in the United States and Canada. This inclusion is enriching and also problematic at points. Most of the General Assembly's resolutions have had primary reference to the religious and social scene in the Unites States, the location of the large majority of the Assembly's North American membership. There are some differences in the culture and legal system of Canada. Therefore, note this from the General Assembly's current *Credentials Manual*:

> The intent of the 2019 edition of the *Credentials Manual* is to provide the definitive standards and processes for the Church of God in the United States and Canada. When references are made to the Internal Revenue Service or 501(c)(3) tax status, the context is the legal and tax systems of

the United States. Similar stances are intended as appropriate within the Canadian legal and tax systems.

There is a significant network of ministry organizations associated with the General Assembly in various ways. They are grouped in three categories, each with a different type of relationship to the Assembly. The resulting organizational picture is as follows:

GENERAL ASSEMBLY

MINISTRIES COUNCIL

Endorsed Agencies   **Affiliated Agencies**

General Director

CHURCH OF GOD MINISTRIES, INC.

Endorsed Agencies
(Covenantal Relationship):

Anderson University
Mid-America Christian Univ.
Warner Pacific University
Warner University
Servant Solutions

Affiliated Agencies
(Coordinating Relationship):

Children of Promise
Christian Women Connection

Other Partners in Ministry
American Indian Council of the Church of God
Hispanic Council of the Church of God
National Association of the Church of God

In addition, there are standing committees of the Assembly, including the Committee on Credentials elected by the General Assembly, with its Chair named by the General Director. It is empowered to act on behalf of the Assembly in all matters related to the ongoing implementation and revision of the Assembly's authorized *Credentials Manual*. It is accountable directly to the General Assembly through the Ministries Council.

2

MEMBERSHIP AND PURPOSES

The General Assembly is self-defined in its formal *Constitution and Bylaws* detailed in chapter 10. Included there are details about its membership and purposes, as well as those of its representative legal body, "Church of God Ministries, Inc." Reads the *Constitution*:

> **MEMBERSHIP.** The membership of the Assembly is intended to be comprised of the widest range of leaders and voices in the movement's constituency (United States and Canada). It includes ministers and representatives of the movement's congregations and recognized ministry agencies. The Assembly retains the right of a voluntary association to define its own membership and decide "when individual ministers or congregations are not recognized by the Assembly as adhering to the general principles to which the Assembly itself is committed." Those general principles appear in chapter three and twenty-one. For details on laypersons as members, see chapter eight.

> **PURPOSES.** This Assembly is recognized as the unified and coordinating expression of the Church of God movement. It is the one venue that brings together the whole family of congregations in the United States and Canada for the purpose of understanding and implementing the Spirit's leading for the movement.

The Constitution and Bylaws of the Assembly defines the Church of God movement as that body of "professing followers of Jesus Christ, members of the Body of Christ, conforming to faith and practice as understood by the light of biblical revelation, in fellowship with one another under the umbrella of the General Assembly of the Church of God in the United States and Canada." It then states the Assembly's particular purpose:

The purpose of the Assembly shall be to further the ends of the Church of God: unity and holiness. As a people embracing Jesus as Lord, the Church of God strives to follow Him as He defined His ministry in Luke 4:16-21. Anointed by the Spirit, the purpose is to proclaim, heal, free, and restore, while conscious of the risks and costs of so doing. The purpose of the Assembly shall be to conduct the general business of the Church and to serve as a forum for the identification, selection, and empowerment of leaders for the Assembly and the ministries and agencies within the Assembly's portfolio.

As seen in the "Functions" chapters of this book, recent decades have seen the General Assembly provide strategic guidance to the ongoing life of the Church of God movement in the United States and Canada.

While not an "ecclesiastical" body in the usual denominational sense, the Assembly does function of the most representative voice of the Church of God movement in the United States and Canada. Additionally, the Assembly now is functioning as a catalyst for helping to create a platform that can serve the Church of God globally. See chapter thirty.

3

A PRIVILEGE AND A LIMITATION

The General Assembly's Constitution and Bylaws identifies it as a "voluntary association" controlled in part by a particular *privilege* and a clear *limitation*. Each of these arise from the nature of the Church of God movement that the Assembly represents and seeks to lead.

A PRIVILEGE RETAINED. The membership of the Assembly is limited to those judged to be "adhering to the general principles to which the Assembly itself is committed." Three such principles have been identified either by direct Assembly resolution or common practice. See the related Assembly resolutions of 1981 and 1985. In brief, the general principles are as follows, with more detail on each found in chapter twenty-one.

1. The **LORDSHIP** of Jesus Christ (Col. 1:15-20; Heb. 1:2-3).

The authority of God's **WRITTEN WORD** (2 Tim. 3:16).

3. The central role of the **SPIRIT OF GOD** who teaches about the meaning of Jesus' lordship, enables a correct reading of the Bible (Jn. 14:26), and inspires the proper manner of implementing the life and ministry of the church.

Jesus said that his Spirit would teach us all things (Jn. 14:26). All that the Spirit teaches is rooted in the lordship of Jesus and consistent with the revealed and written Word of God. Reports the Yokefellow Statement, developed under the supervision of the General Assembly in 1974:

We covenant together that we will stress through every available channel

9

the crucial importance of responsible study and exposition of the Holy Scriptures in all of our preaching and teaching, with particular emphasis upon the centrality of Jesus Christ in his body, the Church, and upon the fulfillment of his mission in the world.

The goal of a congregation of Jesus' people, then, is to be a fellowship grounded in biblical revelation and coming alive in God's Spirit. Jesus told his disciples that they would do many wonderful things in his name, but first they were to wait for power from on high (Lk. 24:49). The effectiveness of the church comes not from human agency or superior programming but . . .

- from the power of God at work;

- from submitting to the lordship of Christ;

- from honoring the authority of God's Word;

- from allowing the Spirit of Christ to live within,

- teach, and minister through humble believers.

Jesus is to be the subject and the biblical revelation the central source of coming to know the Christ. As the Dialogue on Internal Unity would affirm in January, 1981, the Bible is fully trustworthy, the Holy Spirit's guidance is necessary for its proper interpretation, and "divergent views of that interpretation do not jeopardize our fellowship." Particular Church of God authors have elaborated on the central role of the Holy Spirit in the church's believing and acting. Among them are Arlo F. Newell and R. Eugene Sterner.

A LIMITATION HONORED

The Assembly's Constitution and Bylaws say that the Assembly shall not "exercise ecclesiastical jurisdiction or authority over the Church of God in general or over individual congregations in particular." The Church of God movement features a congregational form of polity where each congregation is "independent," legally speaking, although interdependent theologically speaking.

The Church of God movement has resisted being like denominations that are seen as functioning in ways that usurp the primary governance role of the Holy Spirit. This usurping often is done by humanly determining who belongs to God's family, the church, and by formally defining in detailed and restrictive creeds what church members must believe and how they must act beyond the basics of biblical revelation. "Ecclesiastical jurisdiction," then, means that the Assembly will not function in such a "sectarian" manner in relation to its related ministers, congregations, and ministries.

The 1970s saw the General Assembly give considerable attention to the church's seminary, Anderson University School of Theology and Christian Ministry. In 1979 the seminary authored the *WE BELIEVE* booklet circulated widely in that time of the church's centennial celebration. It concludes with this fitting summary of the identity of the Church of God movement which the General Assembly represents and guides:

> In devotion to Christ as the head of the church, we desire to be a biblical people, a people who worship the triune God, a people transformed by the grace of God, a people of the kingdom of God, a people committed to building up the one, universal church of God, and a people who, in God's love, care for the whole world.

4

A REPRESENTATIVE
VOICE

Where does one look for the best voice that announces the thinking of the Church of God movement? The movement has a strong tradition of singing its theology and sense of calling as a particular people. Its entire theology, not available in a formal creed, can be found in such songbooks as *Reformation Glory* (1923). This prominent ministry of music began with the movement's primary pioneer, Daniel Warner, himself a theologian, poet, and singer. The hymnal *Worship the Lord* (1989) has sought to continue this tradition. Recently, however, there has been the sensed need for a more institutionalized voice, partly because the musical medium of carrying the theology has been largely abandoned by new forms of worship.

A frequent function of the General Assembly has been speaking to the church and/or the public as the most representative voice of the Church of God movement. As the 1960 edition of its *Yearbook* put it: "The Church of God is composed of many people in many congregations scattered all around the world. The General Ministerial Assembly is the most representative body within the Church of God through which its world mission and concern can be expressed unitedly and its worldwide work can be approached cooperatively." Later, the word "ministerial" was removed from the Assembly's name to recognize its growing lay membership.

As part of a 1968 resolution on race relations, the General Assembly stated this: "It is the work of this Assembly to authorize, mobilize, and direct the interests common to our life and work as a church, and the church looks to this Assembly to advise and give direction on the particularly spiritual concerns of church life and work."

See the following chapters and the Index for an extensive record of many of the formal actions and stances of the General Assembly on a wide range of subjects of spiritual, doctrinal, ethical, and missional concern. They are the best judgments of the Assembly in given times and sets of circumstances. They are attempts to authorize, mobilize, advise, and direct the church's cooperative life and work. They come from the most representative voice of the movement as a whole in the United States and Canada.

A Brief History

JOURNEY OF THE GENERAL ASSEMBLY

Today's General Assembly is the result of the growth and increasingly cooperative needs of the expanding ministries of the Church of God movement. Found in chapters four through nine is that history in brief.

The movement began in 1880 and the Assembly was formally organized in 1917. The movement's earliest beginning is found in the biography of its primary pioneer, Daniel S. Warner (Barry Callen, *It's God's Church!*, 1995). The subsequent history of the movement as a whole is found in John W. V. Smith, *The Quest for Holiness and Unity* (1980, rev. 2009 by Merle D. Strege) and in *I Saw the Church* (Strege, 2002). Its teaching tradition is found in *Contours of a Cause* (Barry Callen, 1995).

5

A RELUCTANT
BEGINNING

"It's God's Church!" This is a keynote of the Church of God movement and the title of the biography of Daniel S. Warner, primary pioneer of the movement (Barry Callen, 1995). Warner was reacting to the arrogant denominationalism of the late nineteenth century and championing a bold return to the church's direct control by the Spirit of God. Accordingly, establishing "institutions" of ministry in the movement's life came slowly and reluctantly. Leaders were anxious not to duplicate failures of the denominations.

The first organized ministry was the Gospel Trumpet Publishing Company. Warner was founding editor of its influential periodical, the *Gospel Trumpet*. The first "assembly" of the Church of God movement likely was the one convened informally in 1902 at the Yellow Lake Camp Meeting in Indiana. The ministers present assembled in the men's dormitory and sat around on the beds and talked. The only act of formal organization was the appointment of one man to represent the group in talking to the railroads about the availability of special clergy rates. The railroad required a sponsoring national agency to approve clergy for discounted rail travel. Accordingly, this modest assembly became the needed national agency.

This railroad circumstance modeled much to follow. The ministers faced the reality that they could not do the work of the Lord effectively when they were unorganized and trying to function spontaneously in a highly organized society. They would organize, but only reluctantly and as needed, using the often-stated justification that they were organizing the *work* of the church, never the *church itself.*

Such Yellow Creek assembly gatherings were only a beginning. Soon, larger in numbers of ministers and less informal, the most prominent assembly became the one convening annually at the camp meeting in Anderson, Indiana. That assembly began when the Gospel Trumpet Company moved to Anderson from Moundsville, West Virginia, in 1906. It acted in 1917 to organize itself formally as the "General Ministerial Assembly," with only ordained ministers given the right to vote. Pastor E. A. Reardon was elected as founding Chair.

To form a substantive initial agenda, the Gospel Trumpet Company voluntarily submitted a slate of nominees for membership of the company's governing board, thus ending its self-perpetuating nature. This submission gave the body of ministers a feeling of significant participation in that prominent publishing ministry and set a legal and moral precedent for future ministry organizations that wished a legal tie to this central assembly of ministers.

These developments in Anderson were unprecedented and soon of concern to some ministers of the movement. After all, having begun as a resistance to the danger of mere humans organizing church life, and thus risking the impeding of the governance of God's Spirit, dare the movement itself now organize?

The June 28, 1917, issue of the *Gospel Trumpet*, the movement's periodical, reported on this organizing event in Anderson and sought to justify a more formalized Assembly. It said that "the business interests of the church are receiving more careful attention than ever before. The Lord has given the ministry a larger vision of our unparalleled opportunities for spreading the pure gospel to the end of the earth. In order to insure a sound financial basis for these increased activities, better business methods are being considered for the future than we have been accustomed to in the past." This reasoning sufficed for most movement leaders.

From its beginning, then, a reluctant beginning, there has been a tension surrounding the Assembly's very existence. Coming to the Assembly directly from the heart of this movement of the Church of God is the struggle between *autonomy* and *authority* in church life. They seem at odds, but they also both seem legitimate and necessary. For more detail on the Assembly's beginnings, see the thesis of Marvin J. Hartman (School of Religion, Butler University, 1958).

6

CREATING ASSOCIATED BUDGETS

Modest as it was at its beginning in 1917, the General Ministerial Assembly soon was a functioning, organized, and ongoing reality. The decade following its beginning saw various ministry boards, agencies, and a school also forming in the movement's life. A problem was quickly obvious because of these developments. Each of the new ministry bodies was seeking to raise operational dollars from the same congregations, a burden the pastors soon wanted ended. To end the practice would require significant and centralized coordination of budgets. That would be new territory approached cautiously. Even so, it appeared to be a functional necessity.

The 1927 Assembly received favorably a plan that called for any ministry having work that was calling for general church support to prepare an annual budget that would be examined by a "General Budget Committee." This committee would "determine the sum to be set as the goal for each individual cause" and then expect "program coordination of all promotional plans." Guidelines were set for the distribution of designated and undesignated gifts.

This new plan of "Associated Budgets" was soon implemented under the supervision of the Assembly. By 1941 it was known as the "World Service Commission," and by 1955 the "Division of World Service." This significant expansion of regulating the "business interests" of church life had come to require a maturing of the Assembly and an expansion of its coordinating influence. The full autonomy of local congregations remained unquestioned, but the authority of the Assembly nonetheless grew because of the experienced need of a growing church and its expanding ministries.

A sampling of the annual dollars raised from the churches and the pattern of their distribution by the General Assembly is found in chapter thirteen.

7

THE ESTABLISHMENT OF A CORPORATE BODY

Daniel S Warner, primary pioneer of the Church of God movement, suffered personally from the abuse of restrictive church "machinery." He vigorously resisted efforts to organize church life and passed on such negativism. Even so, the publishing ministry that he helped found, the Gospel Trumpet Publishing Company, later called Warner Press, was organized and central to the early movement's very life and expansion. Beginning in 1909, with the formation of the first Missionary Committee, the organizational life of the movement began to grow. The growth was cautious, but definite.

The major organizational and related budget developments of the 1920s led the 1930 General Ministerial Assembly to initiate a study of needed reorganization. This in turn led to the formation of a legally established corporation, a formal "business body" responsible directly to the Assembly. It initially would be called the "Executive Council of the Church of God" and be empowered to hold property and manage the general interests of the church on behalf of the Assembly when it was not in session.

By 1980 the responsibilities of the Executive Council were considerable. It was expected to "coordinate the work of the general agencies authorized by the Assembly in their interrelated and cooperative functions, in their promotional and fund-raising activities, and in the services they offer to the church at large. It shall promote the general welfare and cooperative work of the Church of God." Today this body is known as "Church of God Ministries, Inc." It is controlled by a Board of Directors, the "Ministries Council," which is responsible directly to the General Assembly. See chapter ten for more detail on this corporate body.

8

INTRODUCING LAY MEMBERSHIP

Early generations of the Church of God movement were led primarily by ministers. Gifted preachers had the natural platform for leadership. Increasingly, however, it became clear that laypersons had both the gifting and right to participate meaningfully in the processes of movement decision-making.

In 1939 church historian Charles E. Brown warned against the mistake of too great a separation between vocational ministers and laypersons. "The ministry of the New Testament were prophetic persons, and often such as would be counted laymen today" (*The Church Beyond Division*, 183). This is not to say, however, that vocational ministers lack a special calling from God or would not continue to play a central role in the membership of the General Assembly.

The General Assembly initially was called the "General Ministerial Assembly." Its voting membership was restricted to ministers only. In 1958, however, the Assembly redefined its membership to include "laymen who are elected or appointed members of the Executive Council, a subordinate Board, committee, or commission of the Assembly." Then in 1965, noting that seventy-five laypersons were now members of the Assembly, it acted to remove the word "Ministerial" from the Assembly's official name, making it the "General Assembly of the Church of God."

There followed ongoing concern about the limited membership of laypersons in the General Assembly, partly because they provided most of the funding that enabled the Assembly's ministries. An increase in lay members was authorized in 1982. Then in 1991 there was an additional and significant expansion. Every congregation in the movement now could name at least one lay representative (up to four depending on congregational size). Congregational lay representatives, if present in an Assembly session, would function as full voting members. However, for practical reasons presumably, far fewer laypersons than the number qualified typically have participated in General Assembly sessions. See chapter ten for more detail.

9

GOING BIENNIAL, MOBILE, AND ELECTRONIC

It's been a long way from that 1902 informal gathering of ministers at the Yellow Lake Camp Meeting in Indiana to the General Assembly of today. God has been directing as the numbers of ministers and their organized ministries have multiplied. The Assembly agendas have mushroomed from qualifying for railroad travel discounts to coordinating the formalized activities emerging from God's calling on thousands of leaders and the annual need for millions of operational dollars.

An original pivotal point was the formal organization of the Assembly early in the twentieth century. Another eventually would become seen as necessary. The Dialogue on Internal Unity was convened in January, 1981, and called for a study of the General Assembly itself, including the frequency, duration, and location of its meetings. The dropping of "Ministerial" in the name and the inclusion of lay persons in its membership were important change points, but not the only ones needed.

Radical change would come after a long period of self-study in the 1990s led by the Task Force on Governance and Polity (see chapter sixteen). This had been prompted in part by the sense of inefficiency in the national organizational pattern that had evolved, including a series of free-standing agencies, commissions, and endorsed and affiliated agencies. The result was today's Church of God Ministries, Inc.

Another major pivot point of change came in the second decade of the twenty-first century. The General Assembly was experiencing a steady decline in attendance, in part because of younger ministers not seeing the Assembly's agendas having direct relevance for their local churches. Another reason was the fixed Midwest meeting location (Anderson, Indiana) that kept many from ever participating. From as many as 1,000 participants in earlier years, annually in the 1990s some sessions were 500 or less, occasionally making questionable a quorum for conducting business. It finally was decided to leave the Assembly's long pattern of meeting annually and its traditional meeting home in Anderson, Indiana.

In the most recent years, the Assembly has begun meeting biennially in differing locations around the United States in order to involve ever more church leaders engaged in ever more ministries. Even the process of voting has been changed in the wake of newly available technology. When voting time now comes, rather than a show of hands or distributing of paper ballots, digital devices record judgments electronically and allow immediate reports of the results.

With all this change, however, the underlying reality remains the same. God's servant leaders assemble because they sense being one family in God's Spirit and wish to be good stewards of their common callings from God. The General Assembly is now a major biennial gathering central to the corporate life of the Church of God in the United States and Canada. While remaining a voluntary body, the magnitude of the Assembly's work has evolved the need to order its life with care, especially the life of its corporate body, Church of God Ministries, Inc. The following chapters detail the beliefs and actions of the General Assembly and recall a few of the men and women who have given significant leadership to the Assembly in recent decades.

Guidelines

BASIC OPERATION

On the one hand, the Church of God movement came into being as a reform initiative seeking to free the church of a crippling overlay of human organization that tends to obstruct the work of God's Spirit. On the other hand, the many following years have brought ministry challenges requiring elements of organizational life even in a movement like the Church of God.

Chapters ten through fifteen detail the guide-lines of the basic organization of the cooperative life of the Church of God today in the United States and Canada. While increasingly complex, the General Assembly continues to function in light of the ongoing concern that human organization never be allowed to obstruct the work of the Holy Spirit.

10

CONSTITUTION AND BYLAWS

OF THE GENERAL ASSEMBLY
OF THE CHURCH OF GOD (ANDERSON)

As approved, June, 2019

Following is an abbreviated presentation of the Constitution and Bylaws of the
General Assembly. A full set is available on the web site of Church of God Ministries, Inc.

Definitions

1. Affiliated Agency: agency commissioned by Assembly to serve Church in relationship with Church of God Ministries defined by formal Affiliation Agreement.

2. American Indian Council of the Church of God: free-standing agency providing Church of God ministry to American Indian and First Nations communities.

3. Assembly: General Assembly of the Church of God in the United States and Canada.

4. Ballot: a voting instrument that may include, but is not limited to, paper or electronic means.

5. Charter: Constitution and Bylaws of the Church of God General Assembly.

6. Church of God: professing followers of Jesus Christ, members of

the Body of Christ, conforming to faith and practice as understood by light of biblical revelation, in fellowship with one another under the umbrella of the General Assembly of the Church of God in the United States and Canada.

7.   Church: Church of God

8.   Church of God Global Strategy: a department of Church of God Ministries fielding staff abroad and networking with the Church beyond the United States and Canada.

9.   Church of God Ministries: legally incorporated, non-profit corporation formally named Church of God Ministries, Inc. acting on behalf of the Assembly in the pursuit of the Assembly's ends.

9.   Council: Ministries Council.

10. Endorsed Agency: agency commissioned by Assembly to serve Church in relationship with Church of God Ministries defined by formal Covenant.

11. Executive Committee: an Assembly committee of five comprised of the Assembly Chair, Vice Chair, and Secretary, and two elected at-large from the Assembly's membership.

12. General Director: chief executive officer of Church of God Ministries.

13. Hispanic Concilio: free-standing agency providing Church of God ministry to Hispanic community in the United States and Canada.

14. Ministries Council: Board of Directors of Church of God Ministries, chosen by and accountable to the Assembly.

15. National Association of the Church of God: free-standing agency providing Church of God ministry to African-American community in the United States and Canada.

16. Native American Ministries: a department of Church of God Ministries serving the Native American and First Nations communities in the United States and Canada.

17. Regional Pastor: chief officer or employed pastoral staff member of a state, regional, or provincial assembly recognized by Church of God Ministries.

Name and Purpose

1.   The name of this body is the General Assembly of the Church of God.

2.   The purpose of the Assembly shall be to further the ends of the Church of God: unity and holiness. As a people embracing Jesus

as Lord, the Church of God strives to follow Him, as He defined His ministry in Luke 4:16-21, anointed by the Spirit to: proclaim, heal, free, and restore, while conscious of the risks and costs of so doing.

3. The purpose of the Assembly shall also be to conduct the general business of the Church and to serve as a forum for the identification, selection, and empowerment of leaders for the Assembly and the ministries and agencies within the Assembly's portfolio.

4. The Assembly, in the fulfillment of its purposes and responsibilities, has established a legally incorporated, non-profit corporation formally named Church of God Ministries, Inc. and has chosen a Ministries Council to serve as the Church of God Ministries' Board of Directors; the Council will act on the Assembly's behalf when it is not in session.

Voluntary Association and Membership

1. The Assembly is a voluntary association. It shall not exercise ecclesiastical jurisdiction or authority over the Church of God in general or over individual congregations in particular.

2. The Assembly does, however, retain the right of a voluntary association to define its own membership and to decide and declare, on occasion, when individual ministers or congregations are not recognized by the Assembly as adhering to the general principles to which the Assembly itself is committed.

3. The Assembly's membership shall be comprised of those who are professing Christians, committed to living by the light of biblical revelation, and who also fall into one or more of the following categories:

    a.   Ordained Ministers in good and regular standing with their relevant Church of God credentialing authorities.

    b.   Licensed Ministers in good and regular standing with their relevant Church of God credentialing authorities.

    c.   Governing Board Members of all of the Assembly's Endorsed Agencies.

    d.   Officers of the Assembly's Endorsed Agencies who are subject to the Assembly's ratification.

    e.   Governing Board Members of all of the Assembly's Affiliated Agencies.

    f.   Missionaries who are commissioned by Church of God Ministries.

> g. Members of the Ministries Council.
>
> h. Members of Assembly Committees defined in this Charter.
>
> i. Lay members of Church of God congregations designated by their local church as representatives to the Assembly, under the following formula: one for every one hundred people counted in the local congregation's annualized average weekend worship service attendance published in the Church of God Yearbook current on January 1 of each year; such lay members of the Assembly shall have their eligibility authenticated by a written statement (presented to Church of God Ministries) from the sending congregation's lead or interim pastor, before participation is allowed; if the congregation does not have a lead or interim pastor, such written statement must be signed by the congregation's Board chair or equivalent.

Assembly Meetings and Quorum

1. The Assembly shall meet at least once every two years, at a date and time established by the Ministries Council; such date and time of the Regular Meeting shall be determined and posted with at least ten months advance notice.

2. Three hundred members of the Assembly will constitute a quorum for the definitive conduct of business.

3. Voting in the Assembly may be by printed or electronic ballot; voice votes may also be taken.

Standing Committees of the Assembly

1. Executive Committee: the Chair, Vice Chair, and Secretary of the Assembly, together with two other elected at-large members of the Assembly, shall comprise the Assembly's Executive Committee; the Assembly Chair will serve as Chair of the Committee.

2. Business and Leadership Resource Committee: shall be comprised of twelve members: eleven elected from the Assembly, including two from each of five geographic regions of the United States and one from Canada, and the Vice Chair of the Assembly.

3. Bylaws and Organization Committee: shall be comprised of eight

members: seven elected from the Assembly, and the Vice Chair of the Assembly.

4. Committee on Credentials: shall be composed of seventeen members: fifteen elected by the Assembly and the Chair and representative of Global Strategy of Church of God Ministries appointed by the General Director. It is directly accountable to the General Assembly through the Ministries Council. The will act on behalf of the General Assembly in the implementation, interpretation, review and future occasional revision of the Credentials Manual of the General Assembly of the Church of God.

Church of God Ministries, Inc., Ministries Council, and General Director

1. Church of God Ministries, Inc., is the legally incorporated non-profit corporation acting on the Assembly's behalf, in the pursuit of the Assembly's ends. It shall hold title to all of the Assembly's real assets and be led and managed by a General Director.

2. The Ministries Council, comprised of twenty-four voting members, is the governing Board of Directors of Church of God Ministries, Inc., and is accountable to the Assembly.

3. The General Director is appointed by the Ministries Council, subject to the two-thirds ratification of the General Assembly, and shall provide visionary, pastoral, and administrative leadership for Church of God Ministries.

11

THOSE CHOSEN TO LEAD

Most recent years only

Chairs, General Assembly	Years of Service	General Directors, Church of God Ministries, Inc.*	Years of Service
Samuel Hines	1983-1989		
Oral Withrow	1989-1990		
David Cox	1990-1996		
Robert Culp	1996-2002	Clarence W. Hatch	1954-1960
Randall Spence	2002-2004	Charles V. Weber	1960-1971
Vernon Maddox	2004-2006	William E. Reed	1971-1980
Robert Moss	2006-2010	Paul A. Tanner	1980-1988
Randall Spence	2010-2012	Edward L. Foggs	1988-1999
Rebecca New-Edson	2012-2016	Robert W. Pearson	1999-2002
Diana Swoope	2016-2019	Ronald V. Duncan	2002-2013
Timothy Clark	2019-	James Lyon	2013--

*This incorporated legal arm of the General Assembly and its elected Leader, the General Director, have been known by various names over the years.

Robert Moss

Randall Spence

Rebecca New-Edson

Diana Swoope

Timothy Clark

Edward Foggs

Robert Pearson

Ronald Duncan

James Lyon

Leadership in the Church of God functions within a prevailing paradox. The Task Force on Governance and Polity made this significant observation to the 1992 General Assembly. The Church of God has been blessed with exceptional leaders. However, they have had to serve in the face of a limiting irony. There is a church-wide desire for better national processes, although it is coupled to a reluctance to accept more structure.

A jealous regard for local congregational autonomy is prominent, and yet is accompanied by an equally prominent desire for greater accountability to the whole body. There is both the need for and a distrust of strong church leadership. This continues to reflect the staunch anti-denominational beginnings of the Church of God movement.

12

OVERSEEING AGENCY RELATIONSHIPS

Assuring Functional Integrity

According to the 1960 *Yearbook* of the Church of God, the cooperative work of the movement is carried on by duly authorized boards and agencies that help congregations do together what they could never accomplish separately. The General Assembly gives direction and guidance to these boards and agencies in the following ways: Establishment of Policies; Elections; Ratifications; the Right of Review; and the Adoption of Annual Budgets.

The 1977 General Assembly recognized that its own Constitution and Bylaws grants the Assembly the authority "to declare on occasion when individual ministers or congregations are not recognized by the Assembly as adhering to the general principles to which the Assembly itself is committed." It delegated this authority to its Executive Council to exercise in its sole discretion between annual meetings of the Assembly. See chapters three and twenty-one for detail on the "general principles." Today the Executive Council is known as Church of God Ministries.

The 1984 General Assembly established a procedure for the consideration of new executives of related ministry agencies. It centered in the agency involved providing key information on the candidate, to be shared with Assembly members in advance of its session. The information includes qualifications, credentials, spiritual pilgrimage, and doctrinal convictions. Then the 1985 Assembly established a limitation of terms for members of the governing boards of related agencies. No individual is to be nominated for membership who already has served for two consecutive five-year terms until after a lapse of two years.

A range of ministry organizations in the Church of God movement have come into formal relationship with the General Assembly over the decades. They are identified in chapter one and currently are grouped in three categories, Endorsed Agencies, Affiliated Agencies, and Partners in Ministry. Each category carries its own level and pattern of accountability to the General Assembly. The Endorsed Agency group requires a significant covenantal Assembly relationship and currently includes the four universities and seminary of the Church of God located in the United States.

13

DISTRIBUTING DOLLARS AND MANAGING CRISES

Core activities of the General Assembly and its corporate body, now known as Church of God Ministries, Inc., have included (1) creating and implementing a budget for the church's cooperative ministries and (2) managing occasional crises that had church-wide implications.

DISTRIBUTING DOLLARS

The founding of "Associated Budgets" is detailed in chapter six. Following here is a snapshot of the dollars raised and distributed through the priority decisions of the General Assembly.

1990-1991 (numbers rounded)

Total cooperative budget raised was $9,000,000, 60% of which was allocated to Mission (mostly to the national boards of foreign and home missions) and 31% to Education (national board, seminary, and three colleges/universities). The reminder went to various causes and administrative overhead.

1995-1996 (numbers rounded)

Total cooperative budget raised was $11,700,000, 63% of which was allocated to Mission (mostly to the national boards of foreign and home missions) and 31% to Education (national board, seminary, and three colleges/universities). The reminder went to various causes and administrative overhead.

2014 (numbers rounded)

Total baseline budget was $10,215,000, down modestly from earlier years and now reformatted after a major reorganization of the cooperative ministries. Most of this budget was distributed as follows. Church of God Ministries, $3,372,000; Designated by donor, $5,736,000; Higher Education scholarships, $877,000; and the School of Theology, $219,000.

2019-2021

Total budget approved by the General Assembly for 2019-2021 was $20,873,304, or $10,436,652 per year.

There is no program in the Church of God of congregational "taxation" for support of cooperative ministries. All giving is free-will commitment and generosity as God directs. A significant number of congregations give little or nothing to the cooperative ministries at the national level. The distribution of dollars by the General Assembly brings with it some lines of accountability. See above the general pattern of relationships to the General Assembly of endorsed and affiliated ministry agencies and other partners in ministry.

In an attempt to draw additional support, the 2012 General Assembly adopted a resolution on "Expectation of Giving." It encouraged the giving of local congregations to cooperative ministries of the Church of God and suggested guidelines of giving levels. While adopted, this expectation was only a recommendation, not mandatory, and soon appeared to have little if any effect of giving patterns.

Annual giving to the cooperative budget is not adequate to fund the many ministry needs. One way of reaching for the additional resources came about in 2008. The Church of God Foundation was established under the auspice of the General Assembly's Ministries Council to help fund the future ministry needs of the Church of God. This division of Church of God Ministries, the Assembly's corporate body, is the center for planned giving, providing tools for individuals, congregations, and assemblies to leave lasting legacies for ministry support. It encourages life-long stewardship by offering gift planning and management for wills and endowments, charitable gift annuities, and charitable trusts. By 2013 the Foundation was self-sustaining and distributing resources at donor direction and by priority decisions of its Board of Directors.

MANAGING CRISES

On occasion there have been large-scale crises in the church that have required the General Assembly to intervene. Financial instability in particular became severe in several instances, threatening the well-being of the church in North America. Although each crisis was complex in origin, nature, and eventual handling, here are four examples in brief where the involvement of the General Assembly became necessary.

Mid-America Christian University

In the 1980s this university, previously a Bible College, moved its campus from Houston, Texas, to Oklahoma City, Oklahoma. Considerable debt was involved for the new campus facilities and its repayment was largely dependent on a successful sale of the Texas property. Soon, however, there was a major financial crisis because the oil market in Texas hit bottom and the school's property there failed to sell. Eventually the General Assembly oversaw the launching of a "Giant Leap Campaign" that generated about $400,000 of emergency funds that helped save the school for the church. Today this campus is prospering and under capable leadership.

Warner Press

The Gospel Trumpet Publishing Company (later Warner Press) was the original ministry organization of the Church of God movement. Its publications, beginning in the nineteenth century and extending throughout the twentieth, were vital to holding together and educating many generations of Church of God people. Recent years, however, saw the extensive printing operations ended and the 1996 terminating of the publication of the classic church periodical, *Vital Christianity* (originally *Gospel Trumpet*).

Technological advances, marketplace realities, and resulting financial necessity forced these painful changes. Eventually the changes came to include sale of the large facility in which the printing/shipping operations had been housed and in which the offices of the General Assembly's corporate body were housed. Neighboring land was also sold to Anderson University as one way to deal with major debt. The General Assembly's corporate body sought to inform these major and difficult decisions, and continues to carry a significant debt partly because of them.

Church Extension and Home Missions

In 2000 this significant ministry agency of the Church of God, active since the 1920s, had certain of its investment practices questioned in public. By 2002 resulting litigation, while bringing no criminal charges, resulted in the Securities and Exchange Commission filing a civil action in federal court. This brought into question the credibility of certain financial practices of this ministry agency and, at least in the minds of some, even practices of the Church of God in general. This legal circumstance forced the General Assembly to give this dangerous circumstance its most careful attention.

In 2003 the corporate defendants of Church Extension and the SEC reached an agreement that required the liquidation of all holdings of this ministry for the benefit of creditors and note holders. One complex result was the status of the many conditional deeds of local congregational properties naming this Board as beneficiary. This circumstance was still demanding the time of the General Assembly in 2019. See chapter twenty.

Warner Auditorium

In 1918 a large wooden tabernacle was built on the church grounds in Anderson, Indiana, and for generations was the annual worship center for tens of thousands of Church of God people who gathered there for each Anderson Campmeeting. A crisis occurred in 1960, however, when part of the facility collapsed under the weight of snow. The General Assembly rushed to provide a temporary Campmeeting location in Anderson and then the new construction of an architectural marvel, Warner Auditorium. That landmark facility served well before it also faced a lethal circumstance in 2006. Asbestos contamination was found coming from its giant ceiling. The building was razed, the painful ending of an era of the church's life together.

Rather than facing the high cost of another new building, the Campmeeting was moved for a few years to a large facility on the neighboring Anderson University campus. It now convenes every other year in various congregational and convention facilities around the United States.

A "Strategic Planning Conference" was convened in Nashville, Tennessee, in 2006 under the auspices of the General Assembly. It came in the wake of the above programmatic and financial crises. The hope was to plan more wisely and grasp new opportunities that God was providing the church. For detail on this Conference, see chapter sixteen.

14

PROPER MANNER OF HANDLING DIFFERENCES

Differences of perspective are inevitable in church life. Handling well such differences can be particularly difficult in a church body that prizes freedom as a key way of helping to ensure the primary role of the Spirit of God. Christian unity accepts diversity. Nonetheless, there are limits to acceptable thought and action, and there are acceptable ways expressing differences. The General Assembly has sought to establish the ways of differing without creating division or destroying freedom of thought and expression. It has been a narrow path to walk.

Establishing a "Missionary Committee".............1909

An early crisis in the history of the Church of God movement involved the growing network of independent and unsupervised missionary activities. This led in 1909 to the establishment of a "Missionary Committee" to bring some semblance of order to such well-meaning activities that sometimes were overlapping and even contrasting ministries. Leading minister H. M. Riggle allowed his pragmatism to overcome the movement's bias against organization for the sake of the larger good.

While some ministers resisted establishing such a committee, thinking it a step toward "man-rule," E. E. Byrum's desire to put the life of the movement on more sound managerial footing endorsed this development. By 1917 a handful of other strong leaders would choose to launch a school effort in order to put the movement on more sound educational footing. That would be the beginning of what now is Anderson University. On both the missionary and educational fronts, there was resistance to the new developments. These concerns were handled by explanations of their need and trust in the leaders proposing them.

Integrity of General Church Work.....…...
1947 Resolution

The mid-1940s was a time of considerable tension in the Church of God movement. There was open mistrust of the integrity of the Anderson-based agencies of the church. The 1946 General Assembly appointed an investigating committee to determine the truthfulness of such charges. The 1947 Assembly received the report and resolved as follows.

> ➤ We reaffirm our faith in and loyalty to the doctrines, ideals, and objectives which gave birth to this movement;

> ➤ We express our confidence in the boards and general agencies which serve the church at home and abroad under the authority of this General Assembly;

> ➤ We emphatically disapprove of the spirit and methods employed in the attacks made upon the general work of the church as un-christian, unbrotherly, and unfair;

> ➤ We strongly urge our ministers, when faced with problems re-lated to our general work, to handle all such matters through the proper channels and in a definitely Christian spirit.

Acceptable Procedure for Grievances.......1980 and
1985 Resolutions

The 1980 General Assembly sessions included criticism directed at Anderson University, a national agency of the church. They were made public by a provocative "open letter" mailed by a minister to all Assembly members just prior to the convening of the Assembly. The attention of the Assembly finally was directed toward affirming more appropriate ways for grievances to be handled. Thus, the Assembly adopted the following resolution as procedural guidance for the future:

The national agencies of the Church of God are servants of the church and have been brought into being by action of the General Assembly. Each agency is incorporated and governed by a board of trustees duly elected by this Assembly, and answerable to this Assembly. It is likely that some agency decisions will be unpopular. Members of this Assembly must know that they do have a voice and that their voice will be heard. Therefore, an accepted procedure for sharing differences, grievances, and suggestions is needed. The Business Committee recommends that the biblical basis found in Matthew 18: 15-1 7 be the accepted as the norm and procedure.

The 1985 General Assembly heard more criticism directed at another national agency of the church. The Assembly's Business Committee reaffirmed this 1980 action, redistributed it to Assembly members, and urged that it be honored.

Appeals to the Committee on Credentials.......2017 Resolution

The 2017 General Assembly affirmed a new edition of its authorized *Credentials Manual*. It sets the standards and procedures to be followed by all bodies in the Church of God in Canada and the United States doing ministerial credentialing and congregational recognitions for the Assembly. Included in the Manual is a path for appeals of disputed decisions. In section 7.70 is this:

> Church of God Ministries recognizes the validity of responsible action on the part of a properly constituted and recognized Assembly of the Church of God, including actions on matters of ministerial or congregational discipline. Problems arise, however, when ministers, congregations, and even assemblies disagree on the correctness of an action, or when they reach an impasse that blocks any action being taken.

> In such rare instances, the larger church must become involved. An appeal can be made by any party involved to the standing "Committee on Credentials" of the General Assembly of the Church of God (COC). In addressing such appeals, the COC will give priority to the stance of service rather than authority. Its primary role is to effect reconciliation and redemption and to promote understanding and fair practice. On rare occasions, however, it may need to act definitively to settle an issue otherwise lacking a solution.

15

LOOKING OUTWARD FOR PERSPECTIVE

The early "saints" of the Church of God movement resisted being associated with the "sects" of the denominationalized Christian world. Later generations also tended to stay clear of associations with "ecumenical" movements that were seen as championing false approaches to Christian unity. Even so, the movement increasingly became aware that any organization, including those of the Church of God, can benefit from the assessment of an "outside" and "objective" observer.

Between 1987 and 1994 the officers of the General Assembly invited a series of "fraternal guests" to be observers at the annual sessions of the Assembly and then address the Assembly with observations and recommendations. These seasoned church leaders were leaders of the Free Methodist, Nazarene, Mennonite, and Methodist traditions, and were joined by directors of the National Association of Evangelicals and the North American Christian Convention. A composite of their presentations is found in Barry Callen, *Following the Light* (323-326). Here are highlights.

A common observation relates to what David McCord of the North American Christian Convention called "the enthusiastic ethos" of the Assembly. Bishop Clyde VanValin of the Free Methodist Church said, "You celebrate easily and joyously with a distinctive unity within diversity, a sense of real community." One observed, "You show a trust in the integrity of each other without the need of an authoritarian hierarchy." All spoke of the music and worship sessions as particularly inspiring.

Scholar Dennis Kinlaw of Asbury University was enthused by the singing and observed, "You have a sense of loyalty to your tradition. Pay any price to keep it. Don't sanctify the past, but don't lose those roots." He also pointed to the long trail of church history before Daniel Warner and said, "It all belongs to you. Any denomination that is less than a century old is a sect by definition." Noted was the book *Radical Christianity* by Barry Callen that sets the Church of God movement in a larger and older stream of Christian reforming tradition.

Beyond the appreciations, there were questions and challenges. One spoke of the Church of God emphasis on Christian unity, saying that "it is a message we all need to hear expounded and demonstrated." Billy Melvin, Director of the National Association of Evangelicals, put it pointedly. "Why have I not seen more involvement of the Church of God in the organization I represent? I believe the Church of God has something to share with those larger bodies of Christ." One thing to share, he said, is "your beautiful job of involving our Black brothers and sisters and other ethnics and minorities in your fellowship."

One the challenges being faced, one guest suggested, was consideration of whether "too much emphasis has been placed on the independence of the local church without sufficient emphasis on the interdependence of the whole church. Much may have been lost by the passion of the Church of God to avoid the evils of institutionalization." Said the Mennonite Myron Augsburger, "I like your *movement* language. It speaks of something happening, the Spirit of Christ freely moving among us." But B. Edgar Johnson of the Church of the Nazarene cautioned: "There is a problem with lack of structure. Probably some of your expressed fears about structure in the church's life may be carried over from a long-ago problem—maybe a problem in the thinking of the early founders of the Church of God movement that may not exist today."

Following these years of hearing from "fraternal guests," the General Assembly spent a large portion of the 1990s rethinking the structures that had developed in the cooperative ministries of the Church of God ("Task Force on Governance and Polity"). It relied on an outside consultant, Leith Anderson, to assist with the process that ended with a significant reorganization of the cooperative ministries, including the formation of the current Ministries Council and Church of God Ministries, Inc. See Leith Anderson, "Movement for the 21st Century" (April, 1996). As 1999 began, implementation of this major restructuring was underway. It would be a long and complex process, one to which the General Assembly was fully committed.

Meanwhile, the extensive dialogue between national leaders of the Church of God and the Christian Churches/Churches of Christ yielded a series of consensus statements in 1996. The first was the gaining of self-wisdom that comes with viewing oneself through the eyes of others. Namely:

> We have learned that the roles played by the Enlightenment and American Holiness/Revivalism have shaped the theological perspectives of our respective heritages. This awareness now influences our attitude and helps us to transcend certain limitations coming from our histories.

See chapter seventeen for more on this extensive dialogue.

Functions

CENTRAL ACTIVITY OF THE GENERAL ASSEMBLY

Dr. Robert A. Reardon, then president emeritus of Anderson University, had attended sessions of the General Assembly for forty years when asked to share his observations with the 1992 Assembly. He recalled that his father, E. A. Reardon, had been the first Chair of the Assembly in 1917. Noting several tense times in the Assembly's life when difficult issues had been faced, he said this. "I have seen much evidence of the way the Holy Spirit works. This Assembly is a wonderful example of what charismatic church govern-ment is all about."

A key illustration of the Spirit's working through the Assembly has been its enablement of the Church of God movement to assess its circum-stances and determining its future. This often has been done through the Assembly establishing temporary bodies for study and planning purposes. Prominent examples follow. The Assembly also has taken important initia-tives related to the global constituency of the Church of God movement, an arena well beyond its jurisdiction but not its vital concern. For these initia-tives, see chapters 27-30.

16

CONVENING CONSULTATIONS

An occasional action of the General Assembly has been to establish a temporary venue where church-wide thinking and visioning can occur. The church is to be an ongoing family in active conversation about its life and mission in changing times. The Assembly has acted as a catalyst for ensuring such strategic conversations. Following are such temporary venues of key importance.

All-Board Congress and Planning Council.....................1963

On April 30-May 2, 1963, an All-Board Congress and Planning Council of the Church of God was convened in Anderson, Indiana, to facilitate wide discussion on crucial issues then being faced by the movement as a whole. Nearly three-hundred persons participated in this intense and searching experience, including board members of national ministries, select national staff persons, full-time state coordinators, and one representative from each state assembly. In October, 1963, a Findings Committee summarized the results. In part, they were:

> We call for a clearer, more relevant expression of the existing *theological foundations* upon which this movement stands.
>
> We see the need for a rebirth of doctrinal emphasis, starting with the pulpit ministry and extending through all phases of the church's life. Even so, we would hope to avoid arriving at a dry and rigid creedalism which would undermine individuals whose faith is growing in an atmosphere of Christian fellowship and freedom under God.

We recognize the need to maintain and build up a greater *sense of unity* among ourselves, achieving better and more harmonious working relationships. Our witness must begin with a more adequate demonstration of what we teach, remembering that unity is not intellectual uniformity. While as a church we need to know *who* we are, and *why* we are, we should *not be* setting up distinctives in the denominational sense.

We need a strong emphasis on *redemptive fellowship* in the church. Often our acceptance of other denominations and even members of our own congregations has been conditional, based on whether or not they agreed with "Church of God" thinking. Perhaps we have forgotten the great inclusiveness of "being in Christ." People are going to church where they can receive help, healing, comfort, as well as where they can hear the Truth preached.

Evangelism is seen to be at the very heart of the church. However, it is obvious that we are not getting the message to enough people fast enough. Major concern has been expressed regarding our knowledge of the world and its needs. Sometimes the sickness of the world communicates itself to the church more than the church communicates its life-giving message to the world. It would seem that we are using the language and meanings of another day to communicate with a modern and fast-moving generation. We need to say the same old message in new and different terms.

It would seem that our ministry must be concerned with local, state, national, and even international problems of a social nature. Sometimes the ministry of the church is not appreciated because we have seemingly closed our eyes to situations which exist, such as racial segregation. We have not been without our own problems as a movement. Perhaps we need to spend time and prayer eliminating our own problems before we talk too loudly.

We call for an *increasingly adequate structure* to serve as a channel for implementing our mission. We see a need for a broad study of national, state, and local structure in order to strengthen the work of the church at every level in a coordinated way. We feel that increased *lay representation* is called for at all levels.

Consultation on the Church of God........1970

The 1970 Consultation of the Church of God was constituted much like the one in 1963, with representation from the general agencies and state assemblies. It met with full awareness of the 1963 Congress, the findings of which were distributed and discussed in advance by the delegates. An opening presentation on "the state of the church" identified three focal points to keep in mind during the discussions:

> The scriptural and theological base and imperative inhering in the mighty act of God through Jesus Christ which gives the church its very life.

> The social and practical reality of our time when people are hurting and lost and when Christians are called to incarnational involvement.

> The relative and changing position of the Church of God movement within Christendom as it is expressed in fellowship and united witness.

The major work of this Consultation was done in six sections: (1) Social Concerns, (2) Unity, (3) Lay Ministry, (4) Evangelism, (5) Missions, and (6) Leadership. The findings for each were framed by "issues" and "consensus" and then widely studied, with some suggestions put into effect by the participating state and national agencies.

Yokefellow Statement...........1974

The work of the 1970 Consultation on the Church of God was significantly supplemented by the 1974 Yokefellow Statement coming from the gathering of twenty-five state and national leaders of the Church of God movement. They convened for several days at the Yokefellow House in Indiana and gave prayerful consideration to "the specific objectives upon which we feel the attention and resources of the Church of God should be brought to bear in the immediate years leading up to our centennial celebration in 1980-81." They called for and pledged themselves to the following.

They reaffirmed "the reformational role" of the Church of God movement, calling for "re-establishing the biblical root system of our heritage, and thus nourishing those things that draw us together as a people.... We maintain the conviction that this movement represents a force of reformation leadership within Christendom with its emphasis on ecumenicity based on unity rather than on union."

Recognizing a crisis in presently available leadership, they called for the strengthening of ministerial and lay leadership and a calling of the finest young men and women to give themselves to vocational ministry and the quality training it requires.

They called for "programs and processes that are biblically centered for understanding and addressing social ills and injustices. Racist attitudes are incompatible with the Christian gospel of oneness, brotherhood, and love. We must work toward functional and visible unity."

On the structural front, they said that there must be "exploration of the structuring of state, regional, and national organizations of the Church of God in order to more truly express the oneness of the church in the fulfillment of its mission in the world." They went on to "plead for the development of more precise lines of responsibility, cooperation, and communication that will reflect our interdependent relationships." Note below the later attempts at this development, particularly in the work of the *Task Force on Governance and Polity* (1987-1992) and *Project Imagine* (2017-2018).

Dialogue on Internal Unity............1981

The 1980 General Assembly recognized that there existed among the ministers strong differences of opinion on various agency programs and even doctrinal matters. Therefore, it resolved to urge a serious restudy of the theological and doctrinal message of the Church of God movement. The intent was not to prepare a creed or other definitive statements, but rather to hear and re-examine the doctrinal concerns and mission mandates important to the life and work of the movement.

Two sessions of a Dialogue on Internal Unity were convened, one in January and one in December, 1981. The first focused on three issue areas, Biblical, Structural, and Relational. The second focused on three other issue areas, the Priesthood of Believers, Leadership Development in Higher Education, and the Church of God Response to World Issues. Some of the affirmations and recommendations of the dialogues are found elsewhere in this book under related subjects.

Consultation on Mission and Ministry.......1984

During 1983 final plans were made for the major Consultation on Mission and Ministry scheduled for April, 1984. The General Assembly was concerned about the Church of God not seeming to have a definite sense of direction as it prepared to move into the final years of the twentieth century. It was hopeful that the substantial effort being invested in this coming Consultation would result in more than a few generalizations that would not focus and energize the movement's ministries. The coming consultation would work toward a specific goal-oriented plan for the coming years in the life of the Church of God. The resulting goals were grouped under five areas:

Truth—Here We Stand!

Into All the World

Mission—Good News!

A Living Church

Being the Body of Christ

Glossolalia ("Tongues") and the Church's Life...................1986 Report Approval

The modern "Pentecostal Movement" dates from the Azusa Street Revival at the opening of the twentieth century. Its emphases and influence soon were causing leaders of the Church of God movement to react with concern. While not all agreed, the most prominent position seemed to be in line with that of the influential theological leader F. G. Smith who wrote major articles on the practice of "speaking in tongues" in 1914 and 1919.

Smith distinguished between private and public practices of "glossolalia," the private being unintelligible speech designed for strengthening the individual—to be prohibited in public unless interpreted, and the public being intelligible speech designed for upbuilding the body of believers. He opposed the claim of many "pentecostals" that a speech gift is a necessary sign of the baptism of the Holy Spirit. To him and most leaders of the Church of God movement, the necessary sign was holiness, clear evidence of the Spirit's transforming presence in a life. To claim too much for a gift of tongues easily leads to a deceptive fanaticism. Smith spoke persuasively in this way to the General Assembly.

There developed widespread agreement in the Church of God that God equips the church to accomplish its intended life and mission. Gifts of service are given as God chooses. According to the New Testament, there is a "charismatic" gifting of individuals for the good of the whole church. However, the 1985 General Assembly was hearing cries from many members that "pentecostal" individuals or groups were disrupting the lives of numerous Church of God congregations. The supposed gift of "tongues" was spawning ugly and unwelcome congregational divisions.

A year-long study process was set in motion and resulted in a landmark report to the 1986 Assembly. The report was on the subject of "glossolalia in light of Scripture, our historical perspective, and present happenings in the Church of God movement." It was received with appreciation, commended to the church for careful consideration and implementation, and published in the church's periodical, *Vital Christianity*. A few of the proposed church guidelines are as follows.

A gift of "tongues" is listed in the New Testament as one of the gifts which a given believer might receive as God chooses. However, such a gift is not given to all Spirit-filled believers. Which gift or how many gifts a person is given is not a factor in that person's salvation or sanctification. Unintelligible speech in public worship is unacceptable. A gift of tongues should be seen as the least of the gifts because the person who so speaks without interpretation addresses God but does not directly edify to church through the exercising of this gift. Corporate authority over individualistic assertiveness in congregational life is vital. Said the General Assembly:

> Persons who feel that it is important to promote private manifestations or public demonstrations of a gift of tongues in violation of biblical guidelines should not expect leadership positions in Church of God congregations. Corporate authority over individual assertiveness in congregational life is vital. Submission to each other in the Spirit of Christ is a key to harmonious church life.

Task Forces: Governance and Polity, and Implementation.................1987-1997

The 1987 General Assembly established the Task Force on Governance and Polity. It was charged to "undertake a wide-ranging analysis of present governance and polity traditions, assumptions, structures, and relationships; to develop recommendations for enhancing the effectiveness of governance and polity--congregational, state, and national--to the end that mission and ministry are strengthened." This assignment came to stretch over five years. One interim report to the Assembly identified a basic and troubling tension being the one between *authority* and *autonomy*. The 1991 report to the Assembly included several major recommendations, including:

1. A plan for significantly expanding the lay membership in the Assembly;

2. Establishment of a Mission and Ministry Triennial (plan for periodic revisioning);

3. Restructuring the national ministries arena, including a disbanding of the several free-standing Boards and Commissions.

The primary purpose of this proposed major reorganization was to create a more unified approach to cooperative ministry under a more centralized organizational umbrella.

Some recommendations of the Task Force were implemented and others delayed. Progress was later advanced following the results of a major study by consultant Leith Anderson. His 1996 report was titled "Movement for the 21st Century." It noted that his research in the Church of God indicated a strong desire for enabling a more effective future the Church of God movement. Despite the anti-institutional heritage of this movement, he had discovered a widespread perception that the movement had evolved organizationally into much of what it had traditionally opposed. Accordingly, there were calls by the consultant for the Church of God:

To be more of a movement and less of a bureaucracy;

To enable local churches—so that agencies serve the churches rather than churches serving the agencies;

To organize to fulfill the mission rather than to maintain institutions; and

To empower visionary leadership.

In response, the General Assembly established an Implementation Task Force chaired by pastor David E. Cox and overseen by Edward L. Foggs, General Secretary of what then was known as the Leadership Council. The planning of this Task Force was approved by the 1997 Assembly and implemented in 1998. It finally was the conclusion of this intense and decade-long study process to initiate a substantial alteration of the organization of the cooperative ministries of the church in the United States and Canada, particularly by the formation of the present Church of God Ministries, Inc., and its Board of Directors, the Ministries Council.

Governance and operational control of the following ministry organizations and programs were to shift to the new Church of God Ministries body as rapidly as possible. They were the Board of Christian Education, Mass Communications Board, Missionary Board, Board of Church Extension and Home Missions (partially), Publications Board, Church and Ministry Service, and World Service. Robert Pearson was elected as the first "General Director" of the new body, Church of God Ministries.

Credentials Congresses......1948 and 2017 Resolutions

The 1948 General Assembly determined unacceptable the problems associated with the informality and disparity of standards and procedures being implemented in the granting of ministerial credentials. Accordingly, it authorized the creating of a ministerial credentials manual to regularize such standards and procedures. Resistance to standardization, however, delayed the manual's appearance for many years. The means for developing its content eventually became the convening of "credentials congresses."

The first congress met in 1986, leading to the initial edition of a Credentials Manual for ministers and congregations. Additional congresses followed in 1996, 2003, 2006, and 2010, resulting in new Manual editions. Why the multiple editions? The church kept growing, maturing, changing, and finding itself and its leadership in a rapidly evolving culture with fresh challenges, professional expectations, and legal requirements and threats. The ongoing intent has been "to reflect the proper balance between legitimate autonomy and needed authority in the church's life."

The 2015 General Assembly empowered a "Select Committee on Credentials" to establish the most desirable contents of a revised 2017 edition of the Credentials Manual. One component of this Committee's work was to consult with a new Credentials Congress that convened in two sessions in 2016 and 2017. The intent of the resulting 2017 edition was "to provide the definitive standards and processes for the Church of God in the United States and Canada." The 2017 Assembly also established its standing "Committee on Credentials" that would replace future congresses by making future adjustments in the Credentials Manual as necessary and issuing new editions periodically.

Significantly, the traditional voluntary nature of following the Manual was eliminated. The General Assembly took full ownership of credentialing and determined to authorize for implementation only those state/regional/provincial assemblies that fully endorse and employ the approved Manual. Unprecedented, this action was justified in part by the legal necessity of functioning in equitable, uniform, and accountable ways across the United States and Canada.

Visioning Conferences...............1998 and 2002

A "Mission and Ministry Triennial" was projected as a crucial piece of the large new structural package arising from the work of the Task Force on

Governance and Polity (1987-1992). The first such visioning conference was convened in Colorado in the fall of 1998 with 250 participants. Its purpose was to discover God's will for the Church of God as it approached the twenty-first century. The most significant categories of concern identified were:

Leadership Development—need to broaden the existing leadership base and assist Church of God students in the movement's colleges.

Outreach—need to address the issues of technology and global partnerships in missions, evangelism, and church planting.

Unity and Reconciliation—need to narrow the gap between the church's unity teaching and unity practicing, including racial division and ecumenical outreach.

The second triennial convened in Chandler, Arizona, in August, 2002, "to seek divinely-given vision for the Church of God by providing central insights that inform the Ministries Council and other leadership partnerships in determining strategic direction and goals for ministry." The final plenary session highlighted these essentials of a preferred future:

Lifting up Christ (not our movement);

Lifting up the Word of God (not our hymnal or doctrine);

Agreeing to be accountable (autonomy is no excuse for irresponsibility);

Not trying to reinvent everything instead of partnering with others;

Developing healthy leaders who will build healthy churches.

While valuable, such triennial visioning conferences soon were then abandoned because of cost and the inability of ministry program administrators to accomplish in a three-year period the design, implementation, and evaluation of fresh programming arising from new visioning.

Strategic Planning Conference...........2006

One hundred and forty-three delegates gathered under the leadership of the conference host, Ronald Duncan, General Director of Church of God Ministries, and the conference chair, Vernon Maddox, formerly chair of the General Assembly. Duncan keynoted the conference by recalling the recent crises experienced in the church's corporate life [see chapter thirteen] and the secular culture now being faced. He said that future ministry success depended in large part on three **R**s, **R**estoration of key trust relationships among church leadership, **R**eturning to the basics of the New Testament church, and **R**enewal of collaborative ministries.

Accordingly, the conference's central goal was to address the primary strategic questions understood to then be facing the Church of God. They were:

> What should be the biblical and healthy role of leadership (national, state, and local) for a group of churches that practice congregational polity and the priesthood of all believers?

> How does leadership (national, state, local) honor the traditions of doctrine and governance of such a group of churches, interpret the implications of a changing postmodern culture, and lead the churches forward in reaching that culture?

> What should be the design best suited for harmonious work among national leadership, state leadership, and local churches in a congregational polity system, the design that provides integrated solutions to common needs, challenges, problems, and opportunities?

> How can the vision (missional and relational) of national leadership be best presented to all stakeholders?

After three days of plenary sessions and breakout groups, reported finally were these major learnings and commitments:

> We have rekindled the oneness of the body of Church of God people;

> We have discovered that there is need to determine the core of our Movement's mission for today and then to re-engineer a new Movement DNA focused on that mission;

> We have realized that we have trustworthy leaders and have sensed new hope and desire to be bridge-builders valuing continuing dialogue;

> We are committed to embracing diversity and modeling integrity and connectivity at all levels of church life.

Robert Moss, newly-elected Chair of the General Assembly and its Ministries Council, offered a concluding prayer of commissioning. He urged participants to go forth, keeping alive the inspiration, relationships, and vision of this conference. These was judged a watershed event in the church's ongoing life.

17

ENCOURAGING CHRISTIAN UNITY INITIATIVES

A hallmark of the Church of God movement has been its concern for the necessity of unity among Christians for the sake of effective mission in the world. John W. V. Smith's classic history of the movement is titled *The Quest for Holiness and Unity* (1980, rev. 2009). However, being intentional about achieving and implementing Christian unity has been difficult for a movement suspicious of "organizational" efforts to humanly structure such unity.

For instance, there was concern expressed about the appropriateness of a relationship between the movement and the Federal Council of Churches. Was any such relationship a negation of the Church of God movement's understanding of Christian unity? The 1944 General Assembly established a committee to explore this, but the 1946 Assembly disbanded the committee, explaining that it had not necessarily intended formal joining of this Council and may not even have the authority to commit the movement to such a membership.

To Join or Not?

The Church of God movement began as "come-outers" and not joiners. The 1965 General Assembly, however, established a Committee on Christian Unity (later a Commission) because "the need and responsibility for unity and cooperative work among Christians is so strategic to Christian witness and world evangelism, and the Church of God continues to need a representative group to make contacts, hold conversations, and develop lines of cooperation with other church bodies of similar spirit and concern." We must no longer just preach unity and wait for the Holy Spirit to bring it about.

In the words of the Yokefellow Statement developed under the supervision of the General Assembly in 1974 (see chapter sixteen):

> We maintain the conviction that this movement of the Church of God represents a force of reformation leadership within Christendom with its emphasis on ecumenicity based on *unity* rather than on *union*. We encourage through every means possible the establishing and maintaining of work relationships with other like-minded groups on the national, state, and local levels.

Such encouragement was real although cautiously approached. The 1972 General Assembly had just blocked the church's seminary from being a participant in a grouping of seminaries in nearby Indianapolis, the Foundation for Religious Studies.

The Consultation of the Church of God that convened in 1970 (see chapter sixteen) addressed Christian unity, with the following results:

> *Questions:* (1) Where is the Spirit leading us in intra- and inter-church unity in the 1970s? (2) What is the nature of the unity we seek? (3) What opportunities and obstacles to unity confront the movement? (4) How can the Church of God best contribute to the ecumenical movement?

> *Polarities Recognized:* (1) inclusive vs. exclusive fellowship; social concerns vs. evangelism; "come-outism" vs. cooperative involvement; cardinal beliefs vs. tradition; diversity vs. uniformity. It was agreed that the movement remain a non-joiner but initiate more conversations with other groups, sharing insights on Christian unity wherever doors are open.

Prominent individuals in the Church of God have been active ecumenically and some of its national ministry structures have maintained various working relationships outside the movement. However, caution about cooperative relationships was again evident in 1985 when that General Assembly received and approved a report from its Executive Council. The report encouraged a seeking of intentional inter-church relationships that would activate the movement's message of Christian unity. Criticism immediately surfaced, however, about the appropriateness of relationships with bodies like the World Council of Churches and National Council of Churches in the United States, both said to promote beliefs and public policies contrary to the heritage of the Church of God movement. Guilt by such association was to be avoided.

A committee was commissioned to study related details and then report to the 1988 Assembly. The committee spoke of "risks in all sharing relationships," but insisted that "the isolationist alternative would denominationalize the Church of God movement, an alternative bringing its own high price." It proposed a set of relationship guidelines for all agencies accountable to the Assembly. These included the expectation that there should be no formal institutional membership or even active relationship with any ministry body not "committed publicly to the divinity and lordship of Jesus Christ."

Regardless of the Risks

These 1988 restrictive guidelines were intended to protect but not impede the call to expand voluntary relationships with church groups outside the Church of God movement. After all, the 1985 report to the Assembly had recalled that the Church of God movement historically "has affirmed the unity of the Body of Christ as expressed in its many forms, yet one, and for over eighty years has participated in mutually supportive relationships with other communions through its national and state agencies. Therefore, it should seek intentional inter-church relationships through which its own ministries are strengthened and enriched and which provide opportunity for the Church of God movement to live out its message of Christian unity through enriching the entire Body of Christ."

The General Assembly obviously has faced a paradoxical situation. The Church of God exists in part to take initiatives to enhance the functional reality of Christian unity. It also has tended to remain an outsider to organized efforts among Christian bodies seeking such enhancement. While the Church of God has been suspicious of organizational approaches to Christian unity, a few key leaders have been very involved regardless of the risks. Included have been John W. V. Smith, Gilbert W. Stafford, James Earl Massey, Ronald Duncan, Edward Foggs, Jim Lyon, and Barry Callen, founding editor of Aldersgate Press of the Wesleyan Holiness Connection.

See the essay by Gilbert Stafford in *Following Our Lord* (Callen, 2008, 353ff) and the collection of lifetime writings and ecumenical relationships of James Earl Massey in *Views from the Mountain* (eds., Callen and DeYoung, 2018). Ongoing support of the Wesleyan Holiness Connection has been given by Church of God Ministries. In 2012 the General Assembly approved the Church of God officially recognizing the Global Wesleyan Alliance that seeks practical ways to interrelate several church bodies in the Wesleyan-Holiness tradition, one shared by the Church of God movement. Ronald Duncan of the Church of God has served as this body's executive director.

The issue extends beyond enhancement of appropriate relationships between the Church of God movement and other bodies of believers. There also is the challenge of better relating numerous groups within the movement itself. The 1974 Yokefellow Statement recognized the local congregation as the primary unit of ministry and outreach for fulfilling the church's mission in the world. It went on, however, to plead for "the development of more precise lines of responsibility, cooperation, and communication between the local, state, and national organizations of the Church of God that will reflect our interdependent relationships." The movement has feared formal lines of church authority beyond the local congregation but increasingly has come to realize that risking such lines may be necessary.

An Ecumenical Dialogue......1989-1997

The most extensive effort of the Church of God movement to intentionally engage another church body for the purpose of mutual enrichment involved two American-born church reform movements, the Church of God movement and the Christian Churches/Churches of Christ. This engagement began in 1989 and lasted for nearly a decade. It was prompted by the uncomfortable perception that these two bodies were deeply committed to Christian unity and yet tended to do little to bring such about (for instance, choosing to stand clear of the major "ecumenical movement" of the twentieth century). The extensive dialogue between these two bodies has been recounted fully in *Coming Together in Christ* (1997), co-authored by a representative of each group, Barry Callen of the Church of God and James North of the Christian Churches/Churches of Christ.

This "Open Forum" dialogue process has had lasting results, including a few congregational mergers and large numbers of Christian Churches/Churches of Christ clergy entering *Servant Solutions*, the retirement program of the Church of God. News of the dialogue process was published in the major periodical of each body, *Vital Christianity* and the *Christian Standard*. The General Assembly was kept informed, was supportive, and heard a major report titled "What We Have Learned" (see in Callen, *Following the Light*, 347-352). Two "M" words were spoken of often during these dialogue years. "Merger" of the two bodies was never the motive, but "Mission" was, helped through gaining better self-understanding, building richer fellowship, and cooperating in practical outreach endeavors where possible. See chapter twenty-one for the common theological perspectives of these two church bodies.

18

IMAGINING AN IMPROVED FUTURE 2017-2018

The General Assembly has occasionally sponsored serious planning activity in times of transition. For instance, the Yokefellow Statement of 1974 envisioned priorities leading up to the centennial celebration of the Church of God in 1980. The Consultation on Mission and Ministry that convened in 1984 was the most representative and ambitious effort of its kind in the history of the Church of God movement to that time. It focused on the core concerns and strategic goals basic to responsible long-range planning for the church. A key concern identified was as how best to be the Body of Christ together. How can the movement "develop mutually interdependent relationships that enable the church to be effective in fulfilling in mission and ministry? What are the structures that best express our interdependence and how can we develop them?"

The 2017 General Assembly was still seeking an answer to these key questions. The leadership of the Assembly's Church of God Ministries was pursuing two major goals, (1) finding new ways to increase participation and a sense of ownership in national church life and (2) searching for increased organizational efficiency and financial sustainability in the church's complex and relatively uncoordinated life together.

The Ministries Council affirmed the need for fresh exploration of ways to empower unity and accelerate the advance of Kingdom work. It asked the General Assembly to endorse such exploration and affirm the Council's convening of a diverse "Roundtable" of representative leaders to wrestle with the possibilities, inviting all ministers and ministry agencies to join with the Council's exploratory process.

This proposed process was approved as "Project Imagine." Its prevailing assumption was that "the current competitive and largely uncoordinated atmosphere of multiple ministries in the church is unsustainable." The

Director of the General Assembly's corporate body had voiced a similar judgment in March, 1997, as the national ministries of the Church of God were then being streamlined under the new Church of God Ministries, Inc.: "We have confused autonomy, authority, and accountability in ways that often have made them seem incompatible or even mutually exclusive." How could this confusion be ended?

The eventual result of the 2017-2018 "Roundtable" process of Project Imagine focused on two proposed areas of strategic initiative, each designed to move the church beyond "today's fractured approach to Kingdom advance that cannot be materially or spiritually sustained." These initiatives were:

Initiative #1: The formation of a Church of God networking "table," a body of representatives from the neighborhood of ministry bodies in the Church of God (U.S. and Canada). The goal is to have a central point of initiative and coordination that encourages the launching and enhancement of interdependent relationships that honor appropriate autonomy while more actively fostering needed accountability.

Initiative #2: The identification and formation of a pilot region, one that will work to develop avenues of innovation and cooperation between volunteering state/regional offices and Church of God Ministries. Participating assemblies in a pilot region would retain their organizational integrities (control of finances, officers, assets, etc.) but increasingly would work toward more common agendas, shared measurements of success, and greater alignment of efforts.

A cluster of assembles on the West Coast of the United States quickly volunteered to be this pilot project.

19

AUTHORIZING A MINISTERIAL CREDENTIALS MANUAL AND A PENSION PLAN

World War II was a period of great sacrifice for the United States and also one of considerable turmoil and even bitterness in the Church of God movement. Christ had not returned as originally expected and institutions had developed in the movement despite its great concern about avoiding all "man-rule." But cautious efforts to bring corporate order to the movement's cooperative ministries also brought strong criticism from many conservative ministers. They were "watchmen on the wall." Two developments late in the 1940s were additional efforts of the General Assembly to increase this corporate order in spite of the concern that the movement's heritage not be violated in the process.

A Ministerial Credentials Manual…….. 1948 and 2017

The 1948 General Assembly of the Church of God met in this particularly chaotic time in the movement's life. One result was its calling for a *Credentials Manual* to standardize the ministerial credentialing process in the movement. Order, fairness, and safeguards were needed. Given the movement's anti-organizational DNA, however, it would be nearly four decades before that 1948 call was answered in 1986 with the first edition of the General Assembly's *Credentials Manual*. Other editions would follow each five years or so. As with the Assembly itself, the Manual was a voice of wisdom spoken to the church, but followed voluntarily as various segments of the church saw fit.

Eventually, such volunteerism became unworkable. Just like in 1902 with the requirements of the railroads for privileged clergy travel, and in 1909 when the confusion of uncoordinated missionary activity was no longer ignored, now the social environment of North America rendered ethically awkward and legally dangerous uneven and undependable standards and procedures for credentialing clergy. Therefore, the 2015 General Assembly set in motion the development of a new edition of its *Credentials Manual* required for use by all in the Church of God affiliated with the General Assembly.

Two national credentials congresses were convened for the broadest input on the contents of the new Manual (see chapter sixteen on Credentials Congresses). Then in 2017 the Assembly celebrated the successful completion of the task. This new edition of the *Credentials Manual* intended to put biblical foundations into definitional and operational terms for the current recognition and practice of Christian ministry in the Church of God. It attempts to reflect the proper balance between legitimate autonomy and needed authority in the church's life. As directed by the General Assembly, the standards and processes presented in the Manual are intended to be consistent, equitable, unifying, biblically grounded, and necessarily by all credentialing assemblies.

To oversee the implementation and ongoing revision of this Manual, the Assembly proceeded to establish a standing "Committee on Credentials" charged with the implementation, interpretation, review, and future revisions of the Assembly's Manual. This Committee serves the Church of God in the United States and Canada by receiving, addressing, and resolving, on the General Assembly's behalf, the issues that arise in the church's life relating to ministerial credentials and congregational recognitions. Dr. Barry L. Callen, editor of all editions of the *Credentials Manual* beginning in the 1980s, was named founding Chair of the Committee on Credentials.

A Ministerial Pension Plan.........1948

The late 1940s also saw the General Assembly address another matter so important to ministers. Many congregations were small and the Great Depression had left many older ministers impoverished. Some ministers thought that the idea of ministerial pensions was an expression of lack faith in God's provision. Even so, the Assembly made an initial step forward in 1948 by authorizing the establishment of a voluntary retirement plan. With limited participation initially, after the first twenty-five years of the Pension Fund was custodian of $15 million of assets.

The membership of the Church of God movement was growing quickly in the 1950s, as was the "professionalism" of many of its ministers. Beyond the Pension Fund, college education was increasing and a seminary was founded in Anderson, Indiana. By 2019 the retirement program had mushroomed in size and scope, was called *Servant Solutions*, and was serving a growing number of ministers outside the Church of God movement.

20

ESTABLISHING CHURCH GUIDELINES

The Church of God has been a reform movement of Christians dedicated to the priority of the Spirit of God in individual and church life. The polity that fits best such a priority features the independence of local congregations. Often lacking, however, has been church-wide coordination around common goals arising from careful strategic planning by the movement as a whole. Need for such, however, has become obvious at times and the General Assembly has been the only entity available to provide overall guidance.

Chapters 12-14 highlight this growing "guidelines" function of the General Assembly. Following are three additional examples of this function, the first two coming directly from the Assembly's authorized ministerial *Credentials Manual* (2019 edition).

Expectations of Assemblies

The General Assembly of the Church of God recognizes particular state, regional, and provincial organizations (assemblies) in the United States and Canada to be its agents for credentialing ministers and recognizing congregations. The process of organizational recognition involves that organization's inclusion in each new edition of the *Yearbook* of the Church of God.

Recognized organizations necessarily implement the standards and procedures established by the General Assembly as found in its authorized *Credentials Manual*. They seek to be characterized by the General Assembly expectations that follow. The intent is to provide a means of setting forth goals and measurements by which a recognized organization can self-evaluate as it strives to serve its constituents and foster an environment of health and growth for the expansion of the Kingdom of God.

1. Model the Spirit of Christ which embraces truth in love; strives for unity and commitment to all constituents and congregations of the assembly; stimulates fellowship among its constituents and with other Christian organizations that are like-minded and mission focused.
2. Commit to fulfilling the Great Commission through the ministries of their assembly.
3. Function in harmony with the doctrines and teaching of the Word of God as commonly understood by the teaching heritage of the Church of God.
4. Faithfully implement the General Assembly's *Credentials Manual*.
5. Work to enhance the unity and effectiveness of the mission of the Church of God movement at large.
6. Be committed and intentional about developing strategies and vision that foster an environment of multiplication of congregations and leaders.
7. Remain true to the teachings of Scripture regarding biblical marriage, family, holiness, and salvation through Christ alone.
8. Be committed to embracing and fostering a spirit of unity and equality in accord with the definitions and standards that appear elsewhere in this *Credentials Manual* and in related resolutions of the General Assembly of the Church of God.
9. Encourage opportunities for each congregation within the assembly to be a growing and healthy congregation that is lovingly and effectively reclaiming its community for Jesus Christ.
10. Promote opportunities and a healthy environment of support, fellowship, and accountability for each minister and emerging leader to grow in spiritual knowledge, skills, competencies and abilities in their professional and personal lives so that ministry is enhanced and leaders are developed and intentionally multiplied.
11. Engage, develop, and honor within the assembly strong and gifted leadership that reflects the intentional diversity of that assembly and region.
12. Ensure that the assembly and each congregation maintain responsible practices of organizational integrity, including cur-

rent bylaws and budgets, with congregations encouraged to consider conditional deeding to safeguard Kingdom assets in accord with General Assembly guidelines.

13. Ensure that the work of the credentials committee of the assembly functions in accord with the Credentials Manual of the General Assembly and the recognized practices and procedures of the Church of God as directed by the General Assembly, and that the credentialing processes for every congregation and minister are undertaken with respect, equitably, and in a timely fashion.

Attributes of Recognized Congregations

Any congregation that conforms in intent and usual practice to the following attributes may be recognized by the General Assembly as a congregation of the Church of God.

Is a nurturing local body of believers providing fellowship, inspiration, and support to all within its reach.

Is obedient to God's call to mission at home and around the world.

Provides opportunity for growing in Christian grace and equipping for service.

Lives in harmony with the doctrines and teachings of the Word of God as commonly understood by the teaching heritage of the Church of God.

Upholds a lifestyle characterized by holiness, service, and wise stewardship, as taught by the Bible and consistent with established practices of the Church of God.

Is involved in area, district, state, and national ministries of the Church of God, including such joint activities as worship, training, recreation, and mission projects.

Endeavors to live peaceably as pastors and members with one another and their neighbors.

Is supportive, respectful, and nurturing of all deserving overseers, including its pastor(s) and duly elected leaders.

By both prayer and financial support, contributes to the world mission of the church through the cooperative ministries of the Church of God.

Registers annually and otherwise intentionally links itself to the life of the Church of God.

Invites the counsel of the state office, area assembly's credentialing committee, regional pastor/overseer, and/or Church of God Ministries during times of pastoral change or congregational conflict.

Abides by the procedures for calling a new pastor as outlined in the section of this *Credentials Manual* titled "When Ministers Move..." (see section 5.00).

Is governed by the Holy Spirit, giving decisional authority to pastors and lay leaders as one way to allow Christ preeminence in all things.

Calls and retains on a long-term basis only senior pastors who are approved or likely to gain approval by the assembly under whose jurisdiction that pastor resides.

Maintains liability insurance and indicates such during each annual registration. This insurance must include sexual misconduct.

For the safeguarding of Kingdom assets, is encouraged to maintain in its articles of incorporation a conditional deeding clause, with the beneficiary being the appropriate state, provincial, or area organization of the Church of God.

Conditional Deeding of Church Assets......
1999, 2012, 2019 Resolutions

Note the attribute #16 above that should characterize a recognized congregation of the Church of God. From the 1920s until 2002 the Board of Church Extension and Home Missions led the movement's initiatives to safeguard church properties through conditional deeding. Typically it was named beneficiary in the real deeds of local church land/facility holdings.

The 1999 General Assembly stated that traditionally the Assembly has upheld the concept of conditional deeding as a means of safeguarding Church of God property. In 2006 the Board of Church Extension and Home Missions was in the process of a court-ordered liquidating of all its assets, and conditional deeds naming this Board as beneficiary were transferred to the appropriate assemblies of the Church of God. To clarify related issues and ensure that all matters were on record as having the authority of the General Assembly behind them, the 2012 General Assembly adopted a major resolution on conditional deeding.

Continuing issues, including court actions of 2015 and 2017, required an additional addressing of this matter by the 2019 Assembly. It authorized that Church of God Ministries, Inc., in cooperation with the several assemblies, implement a proactive National Campaign for Conditional Deeding. It is to identify congregations with the Board of Church Extension and Home Missions name remaining in their official documents and assist with the needed changes. It also is to encourage congregations with no conditional deeding in place to consider such as a "legacy" action on behalf of the whole church.

Voice

THEOLOGICAL ISSUES

The General Assembly has functioned as the most representative voice of the Church of God movement. It has spoken to the congregations of the movement in the Unites States and Canada, the cooperative ministry bodies responsible to the Assembly, and occasionally has also addressed publics beyond. Found below is a summary of much of that speaking. It is grouped into three main cat-egories for ready reference. See the Index at the end of this book for easily locating subjects addressed and particular resolutions of the General Assembly.

The first category is the Assembly's occasional speaking on theological issues. Although not a creed-setting body, the Assembly has found it necessary to cautiously enter this arena. Higher education matters are included here because the Assembly's concerns have tended to be less educational philosophy and more the interface between the work and gifting of the Holy Spirit and the presence and intent of the church's institutions of higher education. The history of higher education in the Church of God seeks to balance these twin concerns (see Barry Callen's history of higher education in the Church of God, *Enriching Mind and Spirit*, 2007).

21

DOCTRINAL FOUNDATIONS

Staying Grounded

The General Assembly is a voluntary association that is not exercise "ecclesiastical jurisdiction" or authority over the Church of God in general or individual congregations in particular. Nonetheless, it retains the right of a voluntary association to define its own membership and decide when individual ministers or congregations are not recognized by the Assembly as adhering to the general theological principles to which the Assembly itself is committed.

The General Assembly's avoidance of establishing the precise theology of the Church of God movement was tested early. In 1925 Russell Byrum published his major work *Christian Theology*. It departed in certain ways from the teaching emphases of F. G. Smith, then Editor of the *Gospel Trumpet* and self-proclaimed thought leader of the movement. Smith attempted to have the General Assembly adopt a resolution declaring the "standard literature" of the Church of God movement being only works published *prior to 1924*. That dating would eliminate recognition of Byrum's book, establish a doctrinal watershed and, in effect, have the General Assembly take to itself the right to establish a "creed" for the movement. In its wisdom, the Assembly did not pass this resolution.

While the precise meaning of "ecclesiastical jurisdiction" has never been fully defined, the 1977 General Assembly found it expedient to delegate to its Executive Council (now Ministries Council) "its authority to declare on occasion when individual ministers or congregations are not recognized as adhering to the general reformation principles and practices to which the Assembly itself is committed." It went on to declare that its

Constitution should be interpreted as including "authority to find that a minister or congregation is no longer in fellowship and doctrinal unity with the Church of God." The legal body of the General Assembly was thereby empowered in 1977 "to exercise [this authority] in its sole discretion between annual meetings of the General Assembly."

The membership of the General Assembly is limited to those judged by the Assembly to be "adhering to the general principles to which the Assembly itself is committed." Three such principles have been identified either by direct Assembly resolution or common teaching and practice. See the related Assembly resolutions of 1981 and 1985. In brief, the general theological principles are:

1. The **LORDSHIP** of Jesus Christ (Col. 1:15-20; Heb. 1:2-3).

Said the 1988 General Assembly:

> Any inter-church body involved in a relationship with national ministry bodies of the Church of God should be committed publicly to the divinity and lordship of Jesus Christ. He is central to the meaning and mission of the church! An inter-church relationship should not be maintained if that relationship gives support to beliefs and actions which clearly violate beliefs or actions generally held to be true and proper by the Church of God reformation movement. We in the Church of God must be accountable to each other and maintain the integrity of our doctrinal heritage.

This statement is essential New Testament teaching. A current emphasis of the Church of God movement is that "Jesus is the Subject!"

2. The authority of God's **WRITTEN WORD** (2 Tim. 3:16).

Said the 1981 General Assembly:

> The Bible truly is the divinely inspired and infallible Word of God. The Bible is without error in all that it affirms, in accordance with its own purpose, namely that it is "profitable for teaching, for reproof, for correction, for training in righteousness, that the man of God may be adequate, equipped for every good work" (2 Timothy 3:16-17, NAS), and it therefore is fully trustworthy and authoritative as the infallible guide for understanding the Christian faith and living the Christian life.
>
> This Assembly calls the reformation movement of the Church of God to a new dedication to faithful biblical scholarship and proclamation,

based both upon a commitment to its authority as described above and upon a fresh quest for studied insight and divine guidance in the crucial tasks of responsible biblical interpretation, teaching, and preaching; and further

This Assembly states its expectation that all persons and all programs within this reformation movement of the Church of God reflect a genuine commitment to the Bible as the inspired and authoritative Word of God; and finally

This Assembly states its expectation that governing boards and elected officials, charged with oversight of the operational policies of agencies and the credentials of ministers related to this Assembly, will act responsibly and forthrightly in establishing the central significance of the authority of the Bible and in interpreting and implementing the teachings and directives of the Bible in their respective areas of the work of the Church.

3. The central role of the **SPIRIT OF GOD** who teaches about the meaning of Jesus' lordship, enables a correct reading of the Bible (Jn. 14:26), and inspires the proper manner of implementing the life and ministry of the church in each time and place. This central role of the Holy Spirit is basic to the teaching heritage of the Church of God movement and thus of its General Assembly. For more detail, see chapter three.

The General Assembly's 1986 acceptance of a major study report on glossolalia (tongues) was a pivotal theological action. Included among the affirmations of this report was this:

An infilling of the Holy Spirit and an in-depth life in the Spirit are crucial to the maturing of individual Christians and to the accomplishment of the mission of the church in every age. A lack of the power of Pentecost explains much of the emptiness which the current church renewal and charismatic movements are seeking to fill.

On behalf of the General Assembly, Church of God Ministries is active in 2019 with program initiatives under the caption *PENTECOST LIFE*. New materials for congregational and personal use include starters for sermons, Sunday school classes, and fifty days of Pentecost Bible reading. The Spirit of God constitutes, gifts, governs, and sends the church. Focus here is judged crucial.

Characteristics of This Believing Tradition

The paradox of theology being important and yet not formally stated and mandated is seen in one conclusion of the All Boards Congress and Planning Council convened by the General Assembly in 1963:

> We call for a clearer, more relevant expression of the existing theological foundations upon which this movement stands. We see the need for a rebirth of doctrinal emphasis, starting with the pulpit ministry and extending through all phases of the church's life. Even so, we would hope to avoid arriving at a dry and rigid creedalism which would undermine individuals whose faith is growing in an atmosphere of Christian fellowship and freedom under God.

The paradox is also is seen in this from the Assembly's authorized *Credentials Manual* (2019 ed., 31):

> Although the Church of God honors theological freedom within the bounds of biblically-based belief, those to whom vocational credentialing is granted are expected to hold persuasions that are in general agreement with the teaching tradition of the Church of God.

Without mandating theological particulars, the General Assembly certainly hopes to function in accord with biblical foundations of revealed truth and encourage the Church of God movement to remain faithful to its particular theological heritage and sense of calling on behalf of the whole body of Christ.

Although this movement and its General Assembly have resisted developing "denominational" distinctives and mandatory creedal statements that tend to divide God's people, there are clear characteristics of this believing tradition. See especially *Contours of a Cause* (Barry Callen, 1995), *Theology for Disciples* (Gilbert Stafford, 1996, 2012), and *I Saw the Church* (Merle Strege, 2002). In brief, these contours are:

An All-Truth Vision. The Church of God movement stands committed to whatever is true and yields the life of the Spirit. Emphasis is on the whole truth and nothing but the truth as divinely revealed. There is commitment to what admittedly lies beyond the full comprehension of any one tradition within the Christian community. Believers should be open to drawing from all segments of the Christian tradition that evidence God's revelation and the Spirit's presence.

Experiencing the Power. Christianity cannot be reduced to a series of belief statements, however true they may be. The essence of the faith includes experiencing the truth in life-changing ways. There is to be no isolated, merely intellectual, or routinely repeated confessional formulations of doctrine. Beyond right words lies the divine power to illumine the mind and alter life itself.

Truth in Relationship and Action. "Truth" necessarily involves personal apprehension of the saving presence of God that has come to us in Jesus. There must be a personal relationship followed by responsible action. To "know" God is to be related rightly to God through Jesus Christ and to be engaged rightly in God's present purposes. Being doers rather than mere hearers is required for gaining intimate understanding (James 1:22-25). The essence of Christianity lies in experiencing and then witnessing to and actually living the truth revealed by God.

Convictional, Not Creedal. There is to be strong conviction without oppressive creeds that are humanly developed and always limited. Faith is a pilgrimage, a journey guided by the Spirt toward more and more light. Faith's focus should be on the person of Jesus who himself is the truth (John 14:6).

Comprehensive and Idealistic. Christians are to be more lovers of and seekers after divine truth than definers and protectors of the portions of truth they have gained to date. Being pilgrims toward the fuller truth discourages the dominance of restrictive church establishments and the building of walls that divide God's children. The Church of God Movement has always said, "We reach our hands in fellowship to every blood-washed one."

The extensive dialogue of the 1990s between the Church of God and the Christian Church/Churches of Christ yielded a series of statements affirmed jointly by leaders of these two Christian bodies. They give excellent theological perspective consistent with the central commitments of the General Assembly of the Church of God.

We appreciate the value of the historic Christian creeds, but we are unwilling to make any of these creeds a test of Christian fellowship.

We celebrate our common conviction that Christ is the authority for life and belief.

Christ is revealed through the Bible, as interpreted by the work of the Spirit in the context of the community of faith.

We desire to recover for our time the essence of New Testament Christianity.

We recognize the church as the universal Body of Christ. Each local congregation is called to be a manifestation of this one body.

We recognize the importance both of freedom in the Spirit and mutual responsibility among Christ's disciples.

See chapter thirty-two for a proposed list of "theological non-negotiables."

22

MISSION

Being about God's Business

The mission of the church centers in receiving, embodying, and sharing the good news of God in Jesus Christ. Beyond its various business matters, the General Assembly of the Church of God often has turned its attention to the crucial matter of church mission. Examples follow.

Year of Evangelism...........1970 Resolution

The Church of God movement had been invited to participate in a projected 1973 nationwide evangelism thrust, along with other religious communions. The Board of Church Extension and Home Missions of the Church of God had offered its services in initiating the 1973 evangelism emphasis for the movement. The 1970 General Assembly designated 1973 as the *Year of Evangelism* and urged each minister and local congregation to cooperate fully in this program. It saw this concerted effort across many church bodies as a way to make the Christian witness more vital and relevant in American society.

Emphasis on Church Growth...........1976 Resolution

The 1976 General Assembly voiced the need for the Church of God to urgently and aggressively address its attention and resources toward a more adequate fulfillment of the commission given by Jesus Christ to the church. In view was the stimulating of church growth by employing the wide range of tools, techniques, and methods newly available for this central mission task. The Assembly went on record as endorsing this major effort, especially in the four years leading up to the movement's centennial celebration in 1980.

Church Planting............1984 Resolution

The 1984 General Assembly celebrated how God had richly blessed the Church of God movement with substantial congregational growth through the first century of its existence. It noted, however, that there was urgent need for a more intensified effort in planting new churches among Hispanics, Asians, Africans, Arabs, and more than 80 million unchurched Americans. It affirmed that the church is most obedient to her calling when reaching the lost and unchurched of our nation and world, and that planting and nurturing new congregations is biblical and an effective way to evangelize the lost. The Assembly enthusiastically endorsed this thrust in planting new churches.

Urban Mission............1989 Resolution

Noting that a large percentage of North America's population now lives in urban centers, the 1989 General Assembly recalled a significant fact. Early in the twentieth century the Church of God movement had been very active in compassionate ministries through Missionary Homes in more than forty American cities. The Assembly now observed that, unfortunately, numerous Church of God congregations had moved away from core urban centers, "leaving the urban mission of the church to ethnic minority congregations that often face overwhelming needs with impoverished resources."

The Assembly affirmed metropolitan/urban areas of the nation, "in all their pluralism and problems, to be proper places for the Church of God to be on mission." It urged pastors to raise consciousness of this need, national ministry agencies to target these areas and needs, and schools to develop curriculum "to assist students to understand the city biblically, theologically, and missionally."

Today Urban Missions of the Church of God is a grassroots movement of Church of God congregations that exists to shine the light of Jesus Christ into the shadows of America's large cities. It seeks to establish communities of empathy and hope through daycare and after-school programs, infant crisis and youth mentoring services, job training, and community development initiatives.

Vision-2-Grow!..........1992-2000

The mission statement of the Church of God, beginning from the Lord's command "to go" (Matt. 28:19-20), was "to enable persons to experience redemptive love in its fullest meaning through the sanctifying power of the

gospel and to know Jesus Christ as Savior, Master, and Lord." The rationale for the Vision-2-Grow program of the General Assembly, then, was:

> The Church of God has an opportunity to grow, to win more persons to
> Christ and help them find their place in the fellowship and ministry of a
> local church;

> Visionary, courageous, and trained pastoral and lay leadership can be en-
> listed and are essential to growth;

> The Spirit of God is convicting persons of sin and calling the church to be
> intensely involved in ministries of evangelism and to meet other human
> needs;

> The rapid change in the structures of society and in culture provides the
> church with a unique opportunity to proclaim and demonstrate the gospel.

Directed in its initial years by Rolland Daniels and later by Oral With-
row and Joseph Cookston, *Vision-2-Grow!* was a major program effort
of the General Assembly as it looked toward the beginning of a new century. Numerous "re-generation" workshops were conducted and a video
"The Harvest" produced. A goal was that by the year 2000 there would be
225,000 worshippers on a Sunday morning in North American congregations of the Church of God. That goal was reached and celebrated.

SHAPE and CARE

A significant aspect of the church's mission is developing disciples and
seeking to maintain the physical, vocational, and spiritual health of church
leaders. *SHAPE* (Sustaining Health and Pastoral Excellence) has been a
significant program of Church of God Ministries designed to help pastors
to achieve the hallmarks of faithful ministry—spirituality, connectedness,
knowledge, leadership, vison, and personal health.

More recently, *CARE* (Clergy Advocacy and Resource Effort) has been
another key program of Church of God Ministries. It is addressing the economic issues facing pastoral leaders and advocating for them in financial
planning and compensation. Launched by an initial foundation grant in
2016 and guided by Joe Cookston, this program is part of an inter-denomi-
national effort that believes healthy communities require healthy Christian
congregations that, in turn, require healthy pastoral leaders. A major stress
factor for pastors is financial. CARE has partnered with Servant Solutions
of the Church of God to focus on pastors newer to the ministry and to their

boards in providing financial coaching and funding to assist retirement accounts and student loan debt.

CHRISTIANS BROADCASTING HOPE (CBH)

A longstanding evangelistic ministry of the Church of God has been a national radio ministry initially known as the *Christian Brotherhood Hour*. More recently it has continued the "CBH" identity by being known as *Christians Broadcasting Hope.* It now has gained a large international footprint. It partners with indigenous ministry centers to produce evangelistic programming around the world. CBH has become a radio, internet, and social media ministry designed to expand and nurture the kingdom of God. Radio remains the most cost-effective channel for reaching the widest audience worldwide. Regardless of language or culture, God's love is for all. *People To People* is the newsletter sent to all CBH partners with the latest testimonies from around the world.

23

CHRISTIAN UNITY

Maintaining Proper Associations

Winning the lost for Christ is not understood by the Church of God movement to be limited to preaching, holding revivals, staging camp meetings, and sending missionaries. It must include the church being seen as a united body of believers who evidence in practice as well as speak eloquently about new life in Christ. Therefore, the quest for *holiness* and *unity* is crucial to the process of seeking and saving lost souls. See chapter 22 for detail on actions of the General Assembly in this regard.

Early leaders of the Church of God movement usually set the movement over against all church bodies, calling for the true saints who "saw the light" on the true church to avoid the evils of church institutionalism and division and "come out of Babylon." While this separatist call has lessened considerably in the more recent generations, hints of it remain. The Church of God movement still is reluctant to formally join ecumenical organizations. For instance, see the General Assembly's action against the "Foundation on Religious Studies" in chapter 24.

There has been concern expressed about a particular form of inappropriate association, one often called "secret societies." For instance, the 1994 General Assembly spoke against involvement of Christian people in Freemasonry. This organization was judged a "Christ-less religion." By virtue of its secrecy, it was said to "contravene the Christian's open witness." Because of its oath-bound membership requirement, it was judged "not compatible with the Christian's loyalty to Christ."

The tradition of the Church of God is one of resistance to "denominationalism" and a determination to be a reforming "movement," not just another organizational presence on the complex church scene. The resulting challenge has been addressed well by theologian Gilbert W. Stafford

(*Theology for Disciples*, 1996, 2012, 167-68). The church that structures itself "movementally" in harmony with the early Christian movement must intentionally build *networks of interconnectedness* with the whole church. A church that thinks and acts movementally. . .

Is earnestly devoted to the Christian mission instead of being devoted merely to the survival of its own organizational structures.

Is infinitely flexible in its structured life as it responds to the Spirit instead of being stymied in traditional structures that inhibit the accomplishment of its mission.

The General Assembly has engaged the need for the increased visibility of Christian unity within its own ranks. Sometimes the issue has been multiple assemblies within the same state, assemblies divided along racial lines—see chapter twenty-six for a General Assembly action in this regard. Most recently has come the challenge to transcend national and cultural borders to unify more closely the international family of the Church of God. See chapter thirty.

24

HIGHER EDUCATION

Enhancing Divine Gifts

The Church of God movement began as a reaction against human arrogance and self-serving institutions in church life. Accordingly, establishing its own institutions of higher education has come with great caution. Nonetheless, since the movement was strongly *pro-Spirit* more than it was *anti-education*, higher education eventually became a prominent part of church life. Even so, it began very slowly. For a detailed history of the Church of God colleges, universities, and seminary in the United States, Canada, and the Caribbean, see *Enriching Mind and Spirit* (Barry Callen, 2007).

The General Assembly has wanted to make clear that human intellectual achievement, however valuable, should not replace or supersede the spiritual gifts of God's Spirit. Even so, it declared 1988-1989 the "Year of Christian Higher Education" in the Church of God. By then it was able to recall that the movement "has a long and rich heritage of Christian higher education." It called for a sensitizing of the church to the values of Christian higher education and the importance of attending a Church of God college or university.

Equality of the Educated and Uneducated.....
1918 Resolution

The establishment of Anderson Bible Training School in 1917 was seen by some movement leaders as a potentially positive but also questionable event. The 1918 General Ministerial Assembly accepted a report that read in part:

1.   We believe that such a school can be conducted to the glory of God and the welfare of the ministry and church if kept within certain bounds.

2. We believe that no effort should be made to create a sentiment to the effect that young ministers must attend this school in order to secure recognition.

3. It is our opinion that in many cases the education of ministers can best be obtained in those sections of the country where their ministerial work is to be done so that the practical can be more definitely combined with the theoretical. In other words, we do not believe that the Anderson Bible School should supersede or replace other training schools of the church.

4. Students should be left free to choose their own course of study from among such branches as the school provides.

5. No recommendation or diploma should be given any student. Satisfactory gradings in school constitutes no proof that an individual is called of God to preach the gospel. Hence, every student must be left on his own responsibility so that he will not possess in this respect any authority proceeding from this school which will give him an advantage over those ministers who have not attended school. In the Church of God every minister must stand on his own merits and earn his place of responsibility whether educated or uneducated.

6. We believe that the training of ministers in this school should include more than their intellectual development along educational lines. The most prominent feature must be their personal development in spirituality, faith, and the gifts of the Spirit of God.

Commission on Christian Higher Education.......
1952, 1958 Resolutions

The book *Enriching Mind and Spirit* (Barry Callen, 2007) details the emergence and histories of the several Church of God institutions of higher education in Canada, the United States, and the Caribbean. Because of their independence from each other, perceived competitiveness and occasional lack of understanding about them and support for them was coming from the church. The General Assembly authorized a study commission on higher education in 1952.

The 1958 Assembly, now convinced of the need for a standing body with the general purpose of promoting Christian higher education in the Church of God movement, established the Commission on Higher Education. It would meet annually for nearly four decades, bringing together leaders of all the educational institutions in the attempt to promote increased understanding, appreciation, and support for the cause of Christian higher education in the Church of God movement. This Commission (and others) was disbanded in the reorganization of the late 1990s.

Too Many Colleges?.........1964 Resolution

The 1960s saw the colleges associated with the Church of God movement finding it increasingly difficult to remain in operation because of the lack of resources necessary for an adequate program. The 1964 General Assembly insisted on caution, especially when the launching of a new college is contemplated. It said . . .

> It appears evident that (1) at present there are enough colleges to serve the Church of God student population able and willing to attend those colleges; (2) adequate support is not being provided for existing colleges, most of which are struggling financially for their very lives; and (3) new colleges in the Church continually enter the talking-planning stage are presumably designed to meet the needs of a particular geographic area, but generally are without adequate student and financial support necessary for existence and growth. We urge that, in the establishment of any new college, careful plans be developed for financial support and underwriting, recognizing that the costs of maintaining an adequate program at the college level are enormous.

The Church's Expectations Unclear.........1981 Resolution

The 1981 General Assembly accepted with appreciation a major report from the Board of Trustees of Anderson University. In a section identified as "critical issues ahead," there was call for clarification of the relationship between the church and its colleges. It read:

> Historically, the relationship of the Church of God to its colleges has been largely informal and undefined. There has been the relationship created by the election of trustees, the ratification of chief executive officers, budgetary support and general reporting. However, there is little clarity regarding the Church's expectations of its colleges and there has not been a widespread understanding of what constitutes a responsible relationship between a church body and its institutions of higher learning. We urge an exploration of this subject.

The Seminary of the Church…...

1972, 1974, 1976 Resolutions

The seminary of the Church of God, Anderson School of Theology and Christian Ministries, was founded in the early 1950s as a graduate school on the campus of Anderson University. By the early 1970s the seminary was facing low enrollments, rising costs, and an apparent need for revitalizing the curriculum. Its Board of Trustees set in motion a series of changes, including the establishment of the Center for Pastoral Studies and an affiliation with the Foundation for Religious Studies (an ecumenical consortium of theological schools in nearby Indianapolis, Indiana).

In reporting these changes to the 1972 General Assembly, the seminary received appreciative affirmation of most of the changes, but considerable opposition to the consortium affiliation. It included a Roman Catholic school, raising for some the specter of young Church of God ministers being taught by priests carrying out orders of the Pope in Rome. In a close vote, the Assembly called for ending that new relationship. In the years following, the Assembly acted to bring the Anderson seminary into more direct relationship with the Assembly and to increase funding for its operation. The 1974 Assembly voted to increase annual funding of the Anderson campus specifically for the seminary's operation and to begin fundraising to establish an ongoing tuition-aid fund to assist seminary students with the cost of their graduate education.

The 1976 General Assembly agreed to approve the seminary's remaining under the administrative control of the Anderson campus and commended the Board of Trustees for its considerable attention to the needs and relevance of the seminary in the church's life. Having charged the Commission of Christian Higher Education with making an extensive study of theological and ministerial training in the Church of God, the 1976 Assembly received that report and affirmed its several recommendations. One of them was:

> Responsible Christian ministry in today's world is a very demanding task which calls for the most thorough preparation. We propose that the General Assembly recognize seminary training as the normal, the ideal level of initial preparation for the future young minister.

Since this study and recommendation, the church's seminary in Anderson has continued to serve faithfully with its accredited and graduate-level preparation of ministers. The other campuses of the Church of God have evolved their own graduate-level ministerial education programs. While the goal of seminary training as the ideal remains largely unrealized, the current program of *Leadership Focus* is regularizing and enhancing the preparation of all candidates for ordination outside and yet in relation to the educational institutions.

Voice

PERSONAL AND PUBLIC ISSUES

As the most representative body of the Church of God movement in the United States and Canada, the General Assembly often has spoken to the church on a wide range of issues, both personal and public. Its resolution of 2019 offers the general rationale for such speaking and acting. "The church is called to give witness in all arenas, with its ministry of reconciliation addressing all forms of social and spiritual oppression. We have faith in the power of Christ that calls us to ACT—Awaken, Confront, and Transform society by embracing strategies that bring hope through social action."

While the Assembly does not speak for the church in any definitive manner, its speaking to the church and society as a central voice has been of particular significance across the generations. Because of the Assembly's numerous actions, they are grouped here into two categories: 1. Life in Christ—personal conduct, and 2. God's kingdom now—social policies. The Index at the end of the book can quickly locate for the reader any particular subject or person of interest.

25

PERSONAL CONDUCT

Life in Christ

Those receiving new life in Jesus Christ are expected to grow into mature disciples who reflect in their personal lives the ways of the Master. On a few occasions the General Assembly has confronted a particular lifestyle issue and voiced its judgment and expectation.

Use of Tobacco Products..........1965 Resolution

The 1965 General Assembly observed that the Church of God has "actively taught that the human body and mind is the temple of God, to be kept clean, pure, and fit for the Master's use." It has "stood solidly against the use of tobacco in any form." The Assembly noted the report of the Surgeon General of the United States showing scientifically the harmful effects of tobacco, and it lamented "the insidious advertising which seems to make the use of tobacco desirable by glamorizing the stars of the entertainment and athletic worlds."

This 1965 Assembly reaffirmed the church's traditional teaching on the use of tobacco, asking every minister to take a positive stand in discouraging the use of tobacco, to help safeguard our youth, to help church leaders realize the importance of setting a good example, and to lead the church in a redemptive attitude toward those who are victims of the habit.

Homosexual Practice............1979 and 1993 Resolutions

There always are voices arguing that sexual preference is beyond individual control and thus carries no moral significance. The vast majority of Church of God leaders, however, have judged that homosexual practice is unnatural, can be altered, threatens the fabric of society, and is clearly spoken against in the Bible.

Human sexuality is a gift from God that is to be affirmed, celebrated, and practiced faithfully and lovingly, but only within the sacred bonds of marriage between a man and woman. Many difficult and controversial issues have arisen in this regard, some addressed directly by the General Assembly over the years.

The 1979 General Assembly made clear that persons practicing homo-sexuality as a lifestyle, while to be judged persons of worth and deserving of respect, nonetheless are to be seen as persons living in an unbiblical way not compatible with Christian faith. The affirmation of individuals is to be separated from any affirmation of how they may be living.

> WHEREAS we in the Church of God, being an evangelical people, com-mitted to biblical holiness, give high regard to scriptural injunctions against homosexuality, we are also a redemptive body and seek to express love, compassion, and a chaste relationship in Christ for everyone;
>
> BE IT RESOLVED that the General Assembly of the Church of God go on record as affirming our conviction that biblically we believe homosexual-ity is sin. We hereby stand firmly opposed to the licensing, ordination, or approving of persons in leadership actively involved in this lifestyle, and we stand opposed to any instruction in our church-sponsored institutions or the use of curriculum material which accepts homosexuality as either normal, desirable, or Christian.

In 1993 the General Assembly returned to this issue, continuing to judge a homosexual lifestyle destructive to individuals and society. It called on congregations and institutional leaders of the Church of God "to demonstrate love and provide counsel and materials to assist families and persons confused or distressed by homosexual behavior and to bring redemption and wholeness to those persons." It urged all persons inclined toward homosexual behavior "to seek the grace of God and such other aid and counsel as may be conducive to their relief."

This Assembly, having expressed the words of compassion above, nonetheless went on to reaffirm its conviction, already expressed in 1979, that "biblically, we believe homosexual behavior is sin and stand firmly opposed to the licensing, ordination, or approving for leadership of those involved in this lifestyle, and we oppose instruction that endorses or pro-motes homosexual behavior as an acceptable Christian lifestyle."

Glossolalia ("Tongues") and Church Life......
1986 Consultation

The General Assembly, hardly a "liturgical" body in the usual denomi-national sense, has not set guidelines for the proper order of worship in congregational life. In 1986, however, it did speak about an inappropriate use of the supposed divine gift of "tongues" by an individual. See chapter sixteen for detail.

Domestic Violence............1986 Resolution

The 1986 General Assembly recognized domestic violence as a major social problem in the United States and lamented the misinterpretation of the Bible used by some as justification for such violence. It called on the Church of God movement to "break the silence barrier on domestic violence" and engage in "careful interpretation of Scripture, realizing that correct understanding of the Bible affirms the value and dignity of each individual." The Assembly judged violence as an inappropriate means of conflict resolution and called on the church to "find specific ways to provide protection and healing for the victims of domestic violence and for its perpetrators."

Responsible Sexual Behavior.........
1988 Resolution

The 1988 General Assembly addressed the question of responsible sex-ual behavior, focusing especially on a call for sexual abstinence among the young and unmarried. It lamented the fact that "forces in society encour-age sexual intercourse before marriage." Noting the epidemic of sexually transmitted diseases, the Assembly insisted that "premarital sexual inter-course can damage physical, mental, emotional, and spiritual health." It reaffirmed its commitment "to the sanctity of marriage and the reserving of sex for marriage." It called on the church to "train parents and other significant adults for effectively communicating to young people biblical principles, especially those related to sexuality, sexual activity, marriage, and a healthy self-image."

Gender Identity...........2017 Resolution

The 2017 edition of the General Assembly's *Credentials Manual* says that "the standards and processes presented herein are intended to be con-sistent, equitable, unifying, and biblically grounded." When addressing ministerial misconduct requiring discipline, it says that a minister should "live a lifestyle consistent with one's sex chromosomal identity. We believe the Scriptures teach that God has created us individually as male or female."

26

SOCIAL POLICIES

God's Kingdom Now

The Church of God movement has not chosen to wait for a realization of God's kingdom in this world to the time after the return of Christ. Whatever the obstacles or partial success, God's kingdom is to be evident *now*. Being free in Christ, with bodies understood to be temples of the Holy Spirit, Christians should avoid personal practices that are addictive and lead to slavery. The society in general should be encouraged to create laws that mirror God's loving will for human welfare. Accordingly, the Assembly often has spoken on various social issues and policies.

The 1964 General Assembly authorized the establishment of a Commission on Social Concerns responsible directly to the Assembly. Why? Because "there is manifest urgency for the careful and prayerful study of ways in which articulate calls may be given to the congregations for them to carefully consider Christian responsibility in the fields of temperance and general welfare, particularly with alcohol problems, gambling, tobacco, pornographic literature; in areas of peace and world order, particularly with military policy and legislation for conscription, disarmament, and nuclear weapon control; and in the area of human relations, particularly in race relations, civil liberties, church-state relationships, housing, and civic responsibility."

The 1981 Dialogue on Internal Unity announced that "the Church of God has a biblical mandate to be involved in world issues by caring and doing and cultivating greater awareness." The 1984 Consultation on Mission and Ministry then affirmed this goal: "To challenge the Church of God to redemptive action in relation to the social issues of our time."

With this impetus, and often implemented through the Commission on Social Concerns, various issues of social concern and related calls for action would come to the floor of the General Assembly. On occasion, the Assembly, as the most representative voice of the Church of God movement, would decide to speak to the Church of God movement, and sometimes to the larger church and the general public on behalf of the Church of God movement. Following are such stances taken and proclamations made by the Assembly.

Prohibition of Alcohol.........1928 Resolution

In North America, the use of alcoholic beverages is usually avoided by Church of God people because of their widespread abuse and the personal and social damage they cause. See above for the 1965 statement on the use of tobacco products.

The prohibition of the sale and use of alcoholic beverages was written into the United States Constitution as the eighteenth amendment, effectively beginning in 1920. By 1928, however, Prohibition was being challenged vigorously by some prominent politicians, including attempts to repeal the Eighteenth Amendment. The 1928 General Ministerial Assembly of the Church of God spoke clearly. It judged the repeal attempts as "propaganda, a challenge to morality and public welfare." It resolved to urge strict enforcement of the prohibition laws and opposition to any candidate or political party that favors modification of the present prohibition law.

War: Unchristian and Futile.........1928, 1932 Resolutions

Christians live in a world of power and constant warfare. How should they function as servants of the Prince of Peace? Some Christians participate in military service and others cannot do so in good conscience. Both have been constituents of the Church of God movement. While the movement has not been known as one of the classic "peace churches" (Quakers, Mennonites, etc.), it has had an active peace fellowship since the 1930s and has spoken directly to issues of war and peace.

The General Assemblies of 1928 and 1932 addressed this crucial topic of war. In 1928 it spoke sharply against "war as a method of settling international disputes" and declared itself "in favor of every effort being put forward to propagate the principles of peace." In 1932, recalling the terrible loss of life in World War I, with little gained by anyone, the Assembly stated bluntly that "war is unchristian, futile, and suicidal. We will never again sanction or participate in any war."

Rehabilitation and Conscription.........1947 Resolution

World War II was still fresh on all minds in 1947, with many Church of God people having participated on both sides. In the United States, war had seemed inevitable, even honorable. The Church of God movement, particularly Dean Russell Olt of Anderson University, was active in relocating displaced persons in ravaged Europe. The 1947 Assembly spoke on the subject. After a long series of preliminary statements, it concluded with this:

> BE IT RESOLVED that the General Ministerial Assembly of the Church of God, assembled at Anderson, Indiana, June 18, 1947, commend the leaders of our nation for the splendid work of relief and rehabilitation which they have directed; but

> BE IT FURTHER RESOLVED that we register vigorous objection to any plan for peacetime conscription of youth for military training.

Segregation and the Supreme Court........1954 Resolution

Characteristic of the early Church of God movement was a call to freedom from domineering church institutions, a sense of spontaneous joy in the Lord, and the conviction that all believers are equally a part of the one church by the gracious action of God. These keynotes attracted to the movement socially oppressed people, particularly African-Americans. They also granted to men and women equal access to all levels of church leadership. The 1954 General Assembly reacted as follows to that year's major decision of the United States Supreme Court.

> WHEREAS the United States Supreme Court has rendered a decision to end race segregation in the public schools; and this decision brings to focus certain tensions in the areas of employment, housing, transportation, dining, and other public facilities; and the principles of brotherhood and unity of God's children without regard to distinctive racial groups have been commonly taught in our movement; therefore

> BE IT RESOLVED that this Assembly go on record as being in accord with the spirit and intent of the Supreme Court ruling, and recommends to our people: (1) restraint, patience, and humility in meeting this problem of segregation; (2) that they take an active part in study and efforts in their respective communities to find wise means of solving the problems of segregation; and (3) that there be a continuous demonstration of Christian brotherhood and unity on these campgrounds [Anderson, Indiana], and that there be fair and equitable treatment of all peoples regardless of race or economic status.

Federal Tax Funds for Education.......1961 Resolution

The free-church roots of the Church of God movement go back to the European "radical reformation" of the sixteenth century. A key issue then was the preservation of the church's integrity in the face of control by national governments. The church keeps seeking to determine what it means to be *in* the world and yet not *of it* or controlled *by it*. For full explanation of this "radical" church tradition, see *Radical Christianity* (Barry Callen, 1999).

Where is that point where the church must resist government standards and control in order to maintain its own integrity? In the 1960s the General Assembly saw the point of danger being where government funding is directed to church-related education. The 1961 General Assembly noted that in the news there was much discussion about granting federal funds to private education and concluded that such granting would have particular concern for churches. It expressed the following convictions:

> We reaffirm our confidence in and support of the public school system as an indispensable means of providing educational opportunity for all children. We encourage increased resources for their operation, but oppose any grants from federal, state, or local tax funds for non-public elementary and secondary schools.
>
> We are concerned that the historic principle of separation of church and state be maintained and promoted and urge all branches of the government to avoid any infringement of the ideal of religious liberty which would inevitably arise when taxes paid under compulsion by all people are used to aid non-public schools.

Separation of Church and State........1962 Resolution

The following was a formal statement of the 1962 General Assembly:

> In view of the tremendous pressure now being brought to bear on our federal government for subsidies and handouts by the Roman Catholic Church for its parochial school system, it is now apparent that a definite stand needs to be taken by those of us who favor and believe fervently in the separation of church and state. We believe in the basic principle of the sacred nature of man's relationship to God. We do not believe that this can be legislated nor that it should become a part of political jurisdiction, which is a direct possibility if we were to accept government aid for parochial systems.

No Racial Barriers...........
1964 Resolution

Members of the 1964 General Assembly encouraged Christian action in relation to basic human rights, affirming:

We base our stand on the teaching of the Scriptures. God has "made of one blood all nations of men" (Acts 17:26). "For we are all the children of God by faith in Jesus Christ . . . for we are all one in Jesus Christ" (Gal. 3:26, 28). The first of these speaks as to origin, the second as to relationship. We believe that in the Church of God there should be no racial barriers because we are all brethren in Christ.

We believe that man was made in the image of God, that every person is of intrinsic worth before God, and that every individual has a right to the fullest possible opportunities for the development of life abundant and eternal. We believe that these rights are given by God and that the church has a responsibility to defend them and work for their guarantee.

Firmly believing that the New Testament teaching sets forth a brotherhood without racial discrimination, we will work to achieve an experience of fairness and honest love toward all our brethren, free from discrimination based on race. This calls for patience, understanding, forgiveness, and unselfish service from every member regardless of race. The law of love should be the rule by which we live under all circumstances. We, the General Assembly, urge ministers of state assemblies to:

1.   Make special efforts to get ministers of all races to work toward a united expression of brotherhood and oneness.

2.   Attempt to see that persons, regardless of race, are nominated for committees and offices in the state work according to qualifications.

3.   Where there are segregated assemblies, begin the steps which will eventually bring all the brethren into one working fellowship.

Civil Rights Legislation............
1964 Resolution

The 1964 General Assembly spoke clearly about human equality and needed public policy in the United States.

WHEREAS: the Church of God Reformation Movement believes that the principle of segregation based on color, race, caste, or ethnic origin is a denial of the Christian faith and ethic, which stems from the basic premise taught by our Lord that all men are the children of God;

BE IT RESOLVED: that the General Ministerial Assembly of the Church of God, in session at Anderson, Indiana, go on record as favoring the passage of that type of civil rights legislation which will guarantee justice and equality to all our citizens regardless of race, nationality, or religion.

Equal Voting Rights............1965 Resolution

Since the right to choose a place of residence, to enter school, to secure employment, to vote or attend church should in no way be limited by a person's race or culture, the 1965 General Assembly of the Church of God declared its approval of legislation in support of Amendment XV of the Constitution of the United States which guarantees equal voting rights for all citizens in all fifty states of the Union, without any discrimination based on racial, religious, or economic differences.

Joining the Struggle for Civil Rights............1965 Resolution

Since the time for making ringing declarations against racial discrimination has passed, having moved from saying to doing, the 1965 General Assembly encouraged the general agencies of the Church of God movement to take the steps and risks they deem wise and necessary to involve the church more deliberately in the struggle for equal rights. Since the essence of integrity is to demonstrate ideals and not merely talk about them, the General Assembly urges its members to take direct action as a religious duty to do their part in their local communities to see that voting, jobs, housing, education, and public worship facilities are available to all citizens. Each pastor should encourage greater personal involvement on the part of individual Christians in the struggle for racial justice.

Military Conscription and Personal Conscience.......
1966 Resolution

The 1966 General Assembly viewed with deep concern the escalating military involvement of the United States in Asia and the conscription of the youth of the Church of God for military service. It stated:

We believe that war represents our moral failures. We abhor the causes that lead to war. We stand by the teaching and example of our Lord, who taught us and showed us the way of radical sacrificial love. We are thankful to God that we live in a land of basic freedoms whose law makes provision for alternative service by those "who, by reason of religious training and belief, are conscientiously opposed to participation in war in any form." We encourage our young men who conscientiously object to war to engage in such civilian work which contributes "to the maintenance of the national health, safety or interest."

What we seek for ourselves we seek for every citizen of our land--the right of individual conscience which no governmental authority can abrogate or violate. We do not condemn or reject that person who differs with our position or participates in war. We shall seek to follow such persons with a ministry of health and guidance, but this is never to be construed as approval of war. We fully support young men of the church of God who sincerely and conscientiously are opposed to participation in military service. We encourage them to seek the constructive alternatives intended to bring health, healing, and understanding, and which serves the highest interests of our beloved country and of the whole world.

Repenting and Taking Direct Action...........1968 Resolution

The 1968 General Assembly declared that its previous resolutions on the matter of race relations remain as issues of spiritual priority. It further resolved that the national boards and agencies of the church "be directed to make deliberate moves to secure Negro leaders for executive and/or administrative roles wherever and whenever possible, this being a way to show a more truly inclusive pattern for ourselves on the national level. Be it further resolved that this Assembly direct the Commission on Social Concerns to serve the Assembly by preparing aids and guides for congregational use in resolving differences that keep some of our churches racially separate. This Assembly calls upon the Church to repent for the deficiencies and failures as a people on the point of race relations, turning to God for renewal and grace."

An Open-Door Policy...........1968 Resolution

President Robert H. Reardon of Anderson University addressed the 1968 General Assembly and referred to Charles Naylor's hymn "The Church's Jubilee." He quoted the words "reaching our hands in fellowship to every bloodwashed one," saying that the Church of God had in the past expressed an "open-door policy for all races," but that there was need for more positive action. He presented the following resolution which was adopted by the Assembly:

This Assembly call upon local congregations of the Church of God in the United States and Canada to ratify the following declaration and make it known publicly through whatever means possible:

"In accordance with the teaching of the Scriptures, this congregation of the Church of God welcomes fellow Christians without regard to race, color, or national origin, to participate fully and without any reservation in its fellowship and work."

This Assembly also will instruct its Executive Council to place this declaration before every congregation of the Church of God and make public those congregations ratifying it.

Conviction on War and Peace...........1971 Resolution

The Church of God movement is not one of the classic "peace churches" and yet has been deeply committed to peaceful pursuits in world affairs. It has supported a highly qualified corps of chaplains in all branches of the United States military. A paradoxical stance toward participation in the military is seen in this major statement of the 1971 General Assembly—which repeats much said in its related 1966 resolution.

Like all true Americans, we as members of the General Assembly of the Church of God view with deep concern the military involvement and the conscription of our youth for military service. We believe that war represents our moral failures. We abhor war and the causes that lead to it. We stand by the teaching and example of our Lord, who taught us and showed us the way of radical, sacrificial love.

We are thankful to God that we live in a land of basic freedoms whose law makes provision for alternative service by those "who, by reason of religious training and belief, are conscientiously opposed to participation in war in any form." We encourage our young men who conscientiously object to war and participation in it to engage in such civilian work which contributes "to the maintenance of the national health, safety or interest."

We respect the right of each person to arrive at his own convictions. We believe in the principle of freedom of worship and freedom of conscience. We respect the rights of the individual conscience within our fellowship. We have not set up an authoritative creed. Instead, we accept the entire New Testament as our rule of faith and practice. We seek to lead every member of our fellowship to full comprehension and full acceptance of the Spirit of Christ as the guide for all conduct. What we seek for ourselves we seek for every citizen of our land-the right of individual conscience which no governmental authority can abrogate or violate.

We believe that the cause of Christ is best served when the Christian of draft age responds freely to his own conscience. Because we believe this, we support those who take the position of the conscientious objector. At the same time we insist that the conscientious military person has similar privileges and responsibilities before God. We also support that person who differs with our position regarding conscientious objectors and participates in military service. We seek to follow all persons with a ministry of help and guidance, but this is not to be construed as approval of war.

We fervently pray for the leaders of our nation and of other nations, many of whom we believe to be sincerely striving for peace. We pray that efforts by negotiation among countries, through the United Nations and every possible channel, may succeed in bringing peace to our troubled world. We pray for the Church all over the world to continue her rightful role in peacemaking.

Let this statement of conviction be construed by any and all to mean that we fully support young men of the Church of God who sincerely and conscientiously are opposed to participation in military service. We encourage them to seek constructive alternatives intended to bring health, healing, and understanding, and which serve the highest interests of our beloved country and of the whole world.

Refugees.............1973 Resolution

One human tragedy of war is the displacement of innocent persons and the desperation that usually follows. Said the 1973 General Assembly:

RESOLVED: that the General Assembly of the Church of God urge local congregations to search out and discover these refugees and to devise ways and means of meeting their needs by participating with other like-minded groups in discharging a basic biblical imperative; and be it further

RESOLVED: that this resolution and its accompanying document of information be disseminated to state boards of evangelism and to the pastors and official boards of local congregations in the areas where these refugee problems might appear, with an urgent request for serious implementation; and be it further

RESOLVED: that the General Assembly urge individuals in congregations to keep currently informed regarding any major refugee situation in the world and how immediate relief and ultimate rehabilitation can be accomplished as the political situation will allow; and be it further

RESOLVED: that the above resolution with the document, "Refugee Settlement: Persons Outside the United States," be sent to all pastors of the Church of God, with the earnest request that the church be encouraged to study it and other available information, to the end that it might bring

Christian principles governing such matters to the attention of proper governmental authorities, both state and federal, in such a manner that the government and people of the United States might better serve their proper role in the settlement of refugee situations wherever and whenever they might occur.

Women in Church Leadership............1974 Resolution

The Church of God in its beginning, and especially through its early history, actively included both men and women in its ministry. The emphasis was on all disciples being equal in Christ in the spreading of the gospel of redeeming truth as proclaimed by the movement. Women served in many capacities, as evangelists, teachers, musicians, and pastors. However, the percentage of women in leadership roles steadily declined over the decades. For extensive detail on the church's commitment to women in ministry, see *Called To Minister, Empowered To Serve*, 2nd ed., by Juanita Leonard, Cheryl Sanders, and Kimberly Majeski. The 1974 General Assembly chose to speak on the matter as follows.

WHEREAS women are equipped by their Creator to serve in a variety of roles, including that of homemaker, employment in jobs and professions, volunteer work, and full- or part-time Christian service, and whereas God calls women to use their gifts and skills to their fullest potential,

THEREFOR BE IT RESOLVED that more women be given opportunity and consideration for positions of leadership in the total program of the Church of God, locally, statewide, and nationally.

World Hunger..............1975 Resolution

Hunger is certainly one major cause of war and then the tragedy of refugees. The 1975 General Assembly addressed this matter, noting that Christian people in the wealthy nations, especially in the United States, should be influential in bringing resources to help alleviate the current world hunger crisis. This was to be done initially by the Church of God seeking to raise $100,000 for world hunger and disaster relief during the year of 1975-76.

Black Ministerial Education Fund.........1977 Resolution

The 1977 General Assembly sought to assist the education of young African-American ministers in the southern United States. It considered granting agency status to Bay Ridge Christian College for this purpose, but decided on an alternative since the need was national and not merely regional in scope. It established the Fund for Black Ministerial Education to be administered in consultation with representative African-American leaders of the Church of God.

Violence in Home and Society.........1977, 1986, 1992, 1999 Resolutions

The frequency of the issue violence being addressed by the General Assembly indicates its perceived importance. The 1977 General Assembly noted that television in recent years had added "an alarming increase in the use of profanity and violence and the portrayal of life-styles inconsistent with Christian values." It judged this increase "to be detrimental to the well-being of our families--especially our children and youth." It called for the activation of a write-in plan to be launched by all congregations and directed to the television networks and program sponsors.

The 1986 Assembly noted with equal dismay that domestic violence was a major problem affecting families in every economic, social, and ethnic group. It stated that violence is "an inappropriate means of conflict resolution between adult family members" and hoped to find "specific ways to provide protection and healing for the victims and perpetrators of domestic violence." The 1992 General Assembly took a similar action in regard to violence in the form of sexual, emotional, and physical abuse.

The 1999 Assembly addressed social violence in light of mass shootings in public schools. The home and school, it said, should be "a leavening agent for peaceful and harmonious living in society. While not always favorable toward the United Nations on some political matters, it nonetheless noted that the UN was calling for the first decade of the new millennium to be designated "A Decade for a Culture of Peace and Nonviolence for the Children of the World." This Assembly urged Church of God people to cooperate with the worldwide efforts to bring increased peace and non-violence to all cultures and children.

Abortion on Demand...........1981 Resolution

There is among Church of God leaders widespread opposition to the availability of abortion in general and especially abortion on demand. This is based largely on belief that the unborn fetus is a living human being deserving of protection. Christian compassion should be extended both to life before birth and to the new lives thus preserved. Abortion is judged unacceptable in most if not all circumstances.

After years of activity in the United States directed at passage of an Equal Rights Amendment (ERA) to the national Constitution and related decisions of the Supreme Court, the 1981 General Assembly decided to speak on the major social concern of the legal availability of abortion to almost anyone for almost any reason. The Assembly believed that such liberal availability greatly diminishes the moral values of the one seeking abortion, of the whole nation, and of the unborn child who cannot plead its own defense The Assembly action reads:

WHEREAS, the United States Supreme Court has declared unconstitutional all state laws regulating abortion, and has opened the way for abortion on demand for any reason; and

WHEREAS, the rights of the unborn child are being stripped away by reinterpretation of the Constitution by the Supreme Court and opens the door to possible elimination of other unwanted or undesirable human beings; and

WHEREAS, the Bible contains references to God's personal acquaintance with children prior to birth, inferring the fetus has life (Jer. 1:4-5),

BE IT RESOLVED that the General Assembly of the Church of God go on record as opposing abortion on demand, recognizing that the unborn fetus is a living human being and thus should be protected by the laws and Constitution of the United States of America; and the General Assembly urges all congregations to express compassion and concern not only to protect life before birth but to work to assure that the lives that are preserved receive the care, attention, and help that God wants for all persons; to provide family life and marriage education that will foster such a reverence for God-given life that both the causes and consequences of unwanted pregnancies may be diminished.

Nuclear Arms Reduction.............1982 Resolution

The incineration of planet Earth may be imminent! The 1982 General Assembly addressed this tragic possibility because of the threat posed by the nuclear arms race in which the United States and the Soviet Union were principal participants. Planning the future of our global community, said the Assembly, "is begging the question about a future for this nuclear age. The nuclear arms race could end with its destruction of the human race. We believe that the proliferation of nuclear weapons is a sin against the Creator and against His creation."

Because it may be the most urgent moral issue confronting our generation, the Assembly called Church of God people everywhere to fast and pray for world peace, and for global leaders as they make decisions which affect the destiny of the human family. "We welcome the decision of the United Nations to hold a Second Special Session on Disarmament, and we invite concerned persons and groups to join in fervent prayer during those crucial days. We urge that families, pastors, Sunday school classes, youth, and other groups in local churches give serious study to the question of nuclear disarmament."

The Assembly went on to insist that "the nuclear arms race is not our fate but our choice. There is an alternative. No sinister external force or internal political system is imposing nuclear weapons upon us. Today we are playing brinkmanship with a nuclear shootout because of the accumulation of decisions made by our policy-makers elected and supported by voters and taxpayers. The decision about whether or not we go over the brink into a nuclear holocaust will be made by us, not by persons now in kindergarten, elementary or high school. The alternative is the way of negotiation and agreement."

The Assembly concluded: "Our deliberate choice is to be faithful to Jesus Christ and to his gospel of reconciliation. His purpose for all people is life that is abundant and eternal. To place our trust in weapons of mass murder and destruction is irresponsible and idolatrous. We encourage Church of God people to accept our historical imperative to choose life and to find and support alternatives to the nuclear arms race."

Turning the Nation Back to God.......1983 Resolution

The 1983 General Assembly followed its 1961 and 1962 resolutions on the relationship between the federal government and the churches with this:

WHEREAS it appears that our nation is being confronted with the destruction of the principles upon which it was founded, including "our reliance on the protection of Divine Providence"; and

WHEREAS the President of the United States is currently urging government authorities to permit Bible reading and prayer in the schools and to cease the approval and financing of abortion; and

WHEREAS the Church of God Reformation Movement does not believe in the forbidding of the reading of God's Word or prayer to God in public schools and has gone on record as opposing "Abortion on Demand" (1981); therefore

BE IT RESOLVED that the General Assembly go on record, and so notify the President and the Congress of the United States, that this church body does strongly supports the President of the United States, and all concerned members of Congress, in their efforts to turn this country back to God.

Pornography and Obscenity........1984, 1986, 1990 Resolutions

One obvious way society in general was turning away from God was the growing prevalence of pornography and the public tolerance of obscenity. The 1984 General Assembly observed that the pornography industry had grown to such epidemic proportions that family, church, and community values were being seriously threatened. It also observed that the Supreme Court in 1973 had reaffirmed the right of the community to protect its standards. Therefore, the Assembly called for efforts to inform congregations of the seriousness of the problem. It established a Pornography Awareness Week, issued a call to decency, and urged congregations to become involved in plans of action in their own communities.

The 1986 and 1990 General Assemblies continued to give attention to the degrading effects of pornography and obscenity in contemporary culture. Church of God leader Paul A. Tanner became prominent in the struggle to protect the public, especially children, from such perversions.

Integrating Church Assemblies........1986 Resolution

It was observed by the 1986 General Assembly that progress in the area of race relations had been encouraging but still inadequate. The progress was much too slow and the urgency was increasing. Eleven states in the Church of God still had two ministerial assemblies separated by race. Therefore, the Assembly resolved that all state organizations be urged "to bring about full involvement and fair representation of Negro persons according to ability in the offices and boards and committees of the state organizations. Further, where there are Negro and White assemblies still existing, steps be taken to integrate all ratification procedures in all states immediately and state assemblies report the degree of progress toward the integration of assemblies."

As of 2019, nearly all assemblies are racially integrated. The rare exceptions are not because of racial discrimination, but because of tradition, perceived convenience, and/or cultural preference.

Disabled Persons and Older Adults.........
1988 and 1994 Resolutions

The 1988 and 1994 General Assemblies noted the aging of the population in the United States. In 1988 it said that "the Bible affirms old age as a time when persons are able to reflect earnestly on their lives, share wise counsel with others, and develop the deep spiritual resources of their experiences." It celebrated the ministries to older adults already in process and proclaimed 1989 the "Year of Ministry to and with Older Adults."

Then in 1994 the Assembly stated that the Church of God should "seek to avoid any implication, by act of commission or omission, that the disabled person is a second-class citizen." The church as a redemptive body should "seek to express love, compassion, and concern for those who struggle daily with disability and work toward providing total accessibility for all facets of church worship and related activities."

Mental Illness and Health..........1993 Resolution

Millions of North Americans suffer from some form of mental disorder. They tend to be stigmatized and discriminated against by the general society. Their condition presents the church with particularly difficult challenges. The 1993 General Assembly affirmed that "the church is called to engage in Christ's ministry of healing and advocacy on behalf of those who are ill in body, mind, or spirit, and those who are discriminated against, lonely, unaccepted, and neglected."

This Assembly also called on "the clergy and laity of the Church of God to avail themselves of knowledge of the plight of the mentally ill and their families, and of the latest medical and scientific research into mental illness, so as to dispel fear and prejudice." Congregations were asked to "evaluate their ministries among the mentally ill and seek a fuller and more imaginative and compassionate ministry among this sizable segment of our society."

Same-Sex "Marriage"..........2004 and 2014 Resolutions

The 2004 General Assembly noted with dismay the increasing public and legal acceptance of same-sex "marriages." It recalled its previous addressing of homosexuality, identifying it as sinful, and now went on record "as supporting the definition of marriage as the union between one woman and one man." It further encouraged communication of this action to the United States Congress, urging it "to pass legislation to enshrine the historic definition of marriage in United States law."

The 2014 General Assembly built upon this 2004 action by addressing the role of ministers and church facilities in relation to the occasion of a same-sex "marriage." It recognized that legal trends were threatening to bring pressure on a minister who refuses to officiate at marriage ceremonies contrary to biblical revelation. Therefore, it "resolved to reaffirm its traditional understanding of and sincerely-held religious belief about sexuality, marriage, and its related expectation of appropriate pastor/chaplain practice in these regards." Further, the Assembly recommended that all national and local entities of the Church of God consider establishing policies that restrict the use of their facilities for same-sex "marriages." A model policy statement was developed and shared.

Serving Those Lacking Legal Status...........2007 Resolution

The 2007 General Assembly was aware of sharp political debate in the United States on issues of illegal immigration and residence status. It also recalled its previous stances on ministry without discrimination on the basis of race, gender, and ethnic origin. It now applied such non-discrimination to persons without legal status in the society.

This Assembly affirmed that "ministry in the name of Jesus Christ always involves risk, but risk must never be the factor that determines faithfulness to the call of God to serve needy persons—including the stranger, poor, widow, orphan, prisoner, and those who lack legal credentials." On the one hand, Christians "have a responsibility to follow the employment laws of both state and federal governments." On the other hand, "such laws do not excuse believers and congregations from reaching out with a helping hand to those who are in need, regardless of their resident status."

National Day of Prayer...........2010 Resolution

The 2010 General Assembly recalled the long tradition of a National Day of Prayer in the United States, noting the promise of God that those who humble themselves and seek God's face will be blessed with healing in the land (2 Chron. 7:14). It also noted, however, that a judge had recently ruled a national day of prayer unconstitutional. Therefore, the Assembly went on record as supporting the continuance of such a day and urged legislators to uphold its constitutionality.

Human Trafficking...........2014 Resolution

The 2014 General Assembly faced the tragic fact that many forms of human slavery and trafficking exist today, affecting an estimated 30,000,000 people. It noted the call of Christ for disciples to free the oppressed, and it repented "of any way we have contributed to an economy that profits by human trafficking." It called for raising awareness of this awful problem, support for those who have been victimized, and "commitment to freeing the enslaved and oppressed and putting an end to human trafficking."

An ongoing program of Church of God Ministries designed to fight the global scourge of human trafficking began in 2014 and now is called *TRAFFICKLIGHT*. It is "an arsenal designed to arm you right where you are, reclaiming life in Jesus' name." It is a "unified effort of breaking the chains of sexual slavery and reclaiming what Hell has stolen." *Freedom Fight* is a continuing effort to educate the church about the issues surrounding human trafficking and to empower individuals to impact their own communities.

Affirmations of Compassion and Concern.......
2015 Resolution

In observance of the twentieth anniversary of the Oklahoma City bombing, a racially motivated act of terrorism, and in the wake of the fatal shooting of a pastor and church members in South Carolina motivated by the hatred of Black people, the 2015 General Assembly resolved to express compassion and concern in various ways, including:

> We call on pastors and leaders to follow the guidance of the Holy Spirit to live out a counter-cultural lifestyle that works to expose and repent of the sin of racial division and acknowledges the suffering of our brothers and sisters in Christ.

> We pray for healing, repentance, unity and peace, and we plead for God's mercy on our nation and on those who are compliant with the racial violence and racial disparities being manifested in the church and in the systems of this world.

> We commit ourselves as people of Christian faith to envision, strategize, and work toward the realization of a reconciled church, nation, and world. Let us walk together as we boldly stand against every form of racism.

Repudiating the "Doctrine of Discovery" ....2017 Resolution

See chapter twenty-nine for the context and content of this resolution of the General Assembly. It was one of particular concern to the American Indian Council of the Church of God movement.

The Persecuted Church ....2019 Resolution

The 2019 General Assembly acknowledged that "the daily persecution of Christians is a tragic and intensifying occurrence throughout the world." Being called to share the redemptive and reconciling love of God and bear one another's burdens, the Assembly called on the church to do two things. One was to honor the international day of prayer each November by praying especially "for all Christians who experience cruel and inhumane conditions of persecution." The other was for leaders to special make effort to educate the church about today's persecution of Christians. It was observed from the Assembly floor that people of other faith communities are also being persecuted and Christian conscience should also extend to them, Christian or not.

SERVING THE GLOBAL CHURCH

The Church of God, the Body of Christ, transcends the boundaries of all religious organizations, times, and geographic locations. The "headquarters" of God's church is not in Jerusalem (Jn. 4:20-24) or anywhere else in the creation. Even so, beginning in 1906, and especially after the formal organization of the General Assembly in 1917, the administrative center of the cooperative ministries of the Church of God movement in Canada and the United States has been located in Anderson, Indiana. That center remains the home of Church of God Ministries, the incorporated legal and administrative body of the General Assembly. Increasingly, however, the focus is global.

It became customary to identify this movement as the "Church of God (Anderson, Indiana)," although this Christian body is a global movement of people seeking to fulfill God's mission in the whole world. By the 1980s the movement's constituency had become larger outside North America than inside where it originated. This internationalizing trend has increased. The Church of God now identifies itself as "a global movement of people seeking to fulfill God's mission in the world."

These final chapters review efforts of the General Assembly to "lean forward" by bringing functional reality to this global church community. While usually enabled administratively and financially by the church in North America, increasingly the intent has been to assist with the maturation and participation of regional associations and national church structures beyond North America, even envisioning the formation of some kind of "Global Council" of the Church of God, with all participants on an equal footing.

27

STAGING WORLD CONFERENCES AND WORLD FORUMS

All efforts at globalization have transpired against the backdrop of a tradition critiqued by Donald Johnson and Douglas Welch in the 1980 World Forum of the Church of God. Needed, they said, "is a true international partnership in mission. For too long, North America has determined for the whole movement of the Church of God what is to be considered theologically orthodox, missionally appropriate, and structurally acceptable." Being a servant to the global church, efforts sponsored by the General Assembly in North America should catalyze, not colonize, enable but not dominate. The international wing of Church of God Ministries is now called "Global Strategy."

By the 1970s it was obvious that being unified in mission efforts was facing significant obstacles inside North America, let alone worldwide. Several "para-church" mission groups were active and seeking support from the same Church of God congregations. The 1975 General Assembly sought to set guidelines for the operation of such groups. The announced guidelines included periodic reporting to the General Assembly about the finances of para-church mission bodies receiving major support from the Church of God, a schedule of their meetings, and inclusion in their Articles of Association of a provision that, in case of dissolution, would have remaining assets go to the Church of God and not private individuals. The intent was "to review planning and coordination of programmatic concerns."

Addressing such organizational dis-unity in the movement inside North America was difficult enough; achieving it across the globe would be a greater and ongoing challenge. Nonetheless, numerous efforts have been made under the supervision of the General Assembly, beginning with the Assembly recognizing and honoring international church leaders often present as guests at General Assembly sessions in the United States.

With the administrative support of the church offices in Anderson, Indiana, International Youth Conventions have been convened since the 1920s, all convening somewhere in North America. Only since the 1950s have there been international gatherings of the movement's world leaders. The first of these "World Conferences" in 1955 was essentially another youth convention convened in Fritzlar, Germany, after World War II. It highlighted the presence of numerous youth leaders from Germany and the United States. Many wounds of war needed healing and international bonds of friendship created.

Other world conferences were then convened every four years. They were in Germany, Switzerland, Mexico, Kenya, South Korea, Australia, and England, with select international leaders being increasingly included in the planning process and programs. The 1977 General Assembly in North America launched planning for the movement's centennial celebration in 1980. It envisioned the sixth World Conference to convene in conjunction with this major event to be held in Anderson, Indiana, U.S.A. With it would be the inaugural World Forum and the first International Dialogue on Doctrine. Previous World Conferences of the Church of God had brought a unifying effect on the Church of God in many nations, serving to clarify thinking on many crucial issues and broaden understanding and appreciation for persons in the Church of God in other parts of the world. The centennial time was designed to accelerate this process.

The eleventh World Conference and sixth World Forum were convened in Birmingham, England, in 1999 with about 1,500 international participants. Edward L. Foggs of the United States spoke on "Challenges Facing the Church of God in the Twenty-First Century." He highlighted five.

To affirm that which is universal about the gospel of Jesus Christ;

To live out the unity that is given to us in Jesus Christ;

To bring discipline and accountability to our autonomy;

To fulfill the Great Commission in a world increasingly syncretistic in its outlook;

To recruit, equip, and deploy new leaders for a new day.

The discussion following this presentation focused on number three, asking for some centralized global organization of the Church of God to bring more mutual accountability and increased effectiveness in evangelization efforts. See chapter thirty for developments in this regard.

Although the 1999 World Conference and Forum was the last of its type, the need and concern has persisted. One significant follow-up attempt was the "2013 Global Gathering" convened in Anderson, Indiana, just prior to that year's sessions of the General Assembly. Speakers were representatives of the Church of God from Australia, Brazil, Ghana, India, Jamaica, Paraguay, Russia, United States, and Zambia. Session emphases included "Being the Church in a Changing World," "Growing Together by Serving the World," and "Celebrating the Unity of the Spirit." The overall Global Gathering theme was *"Standing Together."*

28

ORGANIZING INTERNATIONAL DIALOGUES ON DOCTRINE

The first International Dialogue on Doctrine of the Church of God was sponsored by Anderson University's School of Theology and hosted by its Dean, Barry L. Callen. It was planned as part of the larger 1980 centennial celebration of the Church of God that convened in Anderson, Indiana, U.S.A. The General Assembly in North America had convened in the early 1970s a consultation on doctrine with the intent not being to develop a creed or definitive statement but to explore biblically and historically the church's nature and teaching. Now a similar effort was begun on the broader international scene.

Late in the 1970s the faculty of Anderson School of Theology had prepared a booklet titled *"WE BELIEVE"* for use during the coming time of centennial celebration. It was decided to use this document as a general discussion guide for the first International Dialogue on Doctrine in 1980. Papers were written by church leaders from India, Trinidad, Italy, and Kenya, edited and distributed by the School of Theology, and studied in advance. Gilbert W. Stafford of the School of Theology faculty began the dialogue with this: "Just because the Church of God has no written creedal statement does not mean that we do not believe much. We have thought very carefully about our doctrinal life. However, our idea of arriving at doctrinal consensus will not work unless there is doctrinal dialogue. That is what this meeting is all about."

Participants in the 1980 Dialogue prioritized their most pressing doctrinal issues. The greatest was "Pentecost and the Church," which became the topic of the second International Dialogue convened in Nairobi, Kenya, in 1983. Then the 1987 Dialogue in Seoul, South Korea, explored "Gifts of the Spirit," with Gilbert W. Stafford convening. The fourth Dialogue occurred in Wiesbaden, Germany, in 1991, focusing on "Sanctification." Leadership was provided by James Earl Massey, then Dean of Anderson School of Theology, with Barry L. Callen, former Dean, taking the lead in the 1995 Dialogue in Sydney, Australia, around the theme "Christian Unity: God's Will and Our Role Today."

These Dialogues were times of serious theological study and exchange among interested thought leaders across the global church. They did not attempt to formulate "official" positions, but did build friendships, trust, and more disciplined thinking on topics of common concern internationally.

29

CONVENING MULTI-CULTURAL CONSULTATIONS

Sponsored by the Leadership Council of the Church of God (predecessor to the current Church of God Ministries), there was convened in Anderson, Indiana, in November, 1993, a "Cross-Cultural Consultation." In attendance were more than one-hundred persons, including Black, Hispanic, Indian American, Middle Eastern, Asian, and White representatives of the church. They were joined by numerous representatives of the various ministry agencies in North America.

The primary purpose of this Consultation was to afford this broadly-based group from a variety of cultural and ethnic backgrounds a forum to discuss hurts and healing, to consider fresh commitment to each other, and to enhance commitment to the common mission of the church. Goals of conversation involved improved communication, intentional commitment to each other, rejoicing in victories won, future cooperative planning, and consideration of new models of inter-cultural ministry.

An action of the 2017 General Assembly faced one longstanding obstacle to the church facing openly and humbly the challenges of multiculturalism. It was of particular concern to the American Indian Council of the Church of God, one of the "Partners in Ministry" of the General Assembly. The obstacle was the "Doctrine of Discovery" dating back to the 1400s, the Age of Discovery that long pre-dated the origin of the Church of God movement. This doctrine represented a church mentality that featured the supposed superiority of European Christianity over indigenous peoples being encountered in newly discovered lands. It was a mentality justifying the domination and harsh treatment of Native Americans. Elements of such domination persist to the present time. Therefore, the General Assembly acted to recall and repudiate this doctrine.

The American Indian Council of the Church of God seeks to reach Native Americans in Arizona, Nebraska, South Dakota, Idaho, and Washington State as they face high rates of domestic abuse, unemployment, suicide, and hopelessness. This Council expressed deep appreciation for this action of the General Assembly.

Meanwhile, important conversations were proceeding in Africa. They were being facilitated by representatives of the General Assembly and were not only cross-cultural but multi-national. The Church of God movement now has significant constituencies in many countries in sub-Saharan Africa. In recent decades they have grown into maturing national assemblies with limited ties to each other and decreasing dependence on the missionary enterprise from North America.

Mike and Heather Webb were deployed by Church of God Ministries of the General Assembly in 2015 as Regional Coordinators of its work in that African region. They immediately began assessing the challenges facing the ongoing work of the Church of God and convened a 2017 meeting of church leaders from nine African countries. The intent was to encourage more relationships, connectedness, and partnership in ministry.

A follow-up meeting in 2018 was historic. African leaders decided to self-identify as a formal leadership body to more effectively further God's kingdom work among and through them. With the key assistance but not domination of representatives of the General Assembly in the United States and Canada, significant progress was now being made to resource, empower, and unify these leaders of the African assemblies of the Church of God. The shape of the new future is coming from the growing vision of African leaders, and its implementation will be assisted by partnership with representatives of the General Assembly in North America.

30

ENVISIONING A GLOBAL PLATFORM AND PERSPECTIVE

The Church of God movement is a global fellowship of Christians intending to take seriously the keynotes of Jesus "that they all may be one" in order that the gospel witness can go "to all the world." This movement's originating vision was that all of the human, the partial, and the non-biblical be shed from the church's life. Believers are to stand together, unified, purified, empowered, gifted, governed, and sent by God's Spirit. Following this vision will bring risk—it took Jesus to a cross. No matter. The church brought into being by God is to be the church of God and of God's agenda in the world.

The 1998 Visioning Conference (see chapter sixteen) had highlighted "the need to address the issues of technology and global partnerships in missions, evangelism, and church planting." But then came the ending of the World Conferences, Forums, and International Dialogues on Doctrine largely because of the tragic terrorism attack on the United States in 2001 and the resulting loss of will and lack of resources for international travel. The need continued, however. A "Global Dialogue" of thirty-two international delegates was convened in Anderson, Indiana, in 2003 to access past international efforts and find the best way forward. This led to "Global Gathering 2013" with the tag line "Standing Together! Being the Body of Christ in a Changing World."

Toward a Global Council of Assemblies

The Church of God movement is now comprised of nearly 1,000,000 constituents scattered globally in some ninety countries and 8,000 congregations. A large majority of these constituents reside outside North America. There is perceived need for more integration and interface, a closer relationship between the various branches of the Church of God family in North America and the world beyond. A pivotal gathering to explore this need and the possibilities was convened in Belfast, Ireland, in June, 2014, enabled by the leadership of the General Assembly in North America and particularly Jim Lyon, General Director of Church of God Ministries.

Assembly leaders reconvened the Belfast Roundtable in the United States in 2015. That conversation honored the generations of Church of God North Americans who had sent missionaries and many millions of dollars and administrative support services to bless the world-wide mission of God. National assemblies and regional structures now have evolved and matured around the world. The present need is to think more collectively, maximize resources, and envision a more unified international family of the Church of God.

The result of these ongoing conversations is envisioned as something like a "Global Church of God Council of Assemblies." Spearheading such a significant effort will require the continuing involvement of Church of God Ministries, the corporate body of the General Assembly in the United States and Canada. Such involvement will be given enthusiastically.

Perspectives for All Church Bodies

The church is called to and enabled by the grace of God to journey together—*unity*—into the very life of God. This journey enables a participation in the divine life—*holiness*—that motivates a sharing of that life with all others in this troubled world—*mission*. While only partially successful in this vital journey, the Church of God movement nonetheless judges that it has been given perspectives worthy of sharing with God's family globally.

From these various international gatherings and hope for a more unified family of the Church of God movement internationally, there also has emerged some general perspectives of the Church of God judged valuable for Christians of any affiliation in any national setting. Every body of Christian believers tends to have its own culture and emphases. These can be enriching to the larger body of Christ's followers if they are held humbly and shared with the intent of building up the body of Christ.

The Church of God movement, now a global fellowship, hopes to share widely several of its own particular perspectives for the fuller health and mission effectiveness of the whole church. It does so humbly, remaining open to the perspectives of other Christian communities. Here are seven such perspectives that the Church of God movement tends to emphasize and hopes to share worldwide.

For the good of the whole church, each body of believers should cherish and share the **particular understandings of biblical truth** that it possesses, while remaining open to being enriched by the understandings of fellow believers. To be resisted are detailed and mandatory creeds that freeze understandings, discourage further learning, and are used as tools of division.

Every body of Christians should focus on **being a movement**, avoiding the pitfall of corrosive church institutionalism. While organizing the church's work is necessary stewardship, claiming biblical finality for any organizational pattern is inappropriate. To be resisted is any "sectarian" spirit.

Bible-based theology is very important, but theology isn't everything. Christian identity and church membership are to be rooted **in Christian experience**, persons being reborn by action of the Spirit. Affiliation with a church body apart from new life in Christ is false church membership and poor theology. To be resisted is mere memorization and repeating of the classic creeds of the church, "orthodox" though they may be.

Christian faith and life must be **Spirit-oriented**. Fearing possible emotional excess must not distract from this central truth of Christianity. The church was born at Pentecost and is to be gifted, empowered, and governed by the Spirit of God, regardless of what organizational plan is employed or creed affirmed. To be resisted, however, is overly standardizing the subjective particulars of "Christian experience."

Unity among all Christians is crucial to effective church mission and will never be achieved by Christians agreeing on all points of theology and practice, or by denominations flowing together into one master church organization. Christian unity is the fruit of **common new life in the Spirit of Christ**. Believers are to serve together as united instruments of the Spirit's ministry.

Expectations of end-time events should be tempered by humility and disciplined by the clear biblical mandate to focus on **the present mission of the church**. We must resist speculations that distract from the ministry tasks and reconciliation possibilities immediately at hand.

What is the mission of the church? The resurrection of Jesus was the beginning of God's ongoing project of infusing this fallen world with **the life of heaven**. The church is to **model and witness** to this new (real) life in the Spirit, making disciples of the Master and assisting with their spiritual maturing and service deployment without racial or gender discrimination.

It is believed that these seven perspectives are biblical and vital for the spiritual health and mission effectiveness of the church in every nation and culture. May God grant these perspectives a constructive role in the future ministries of the Body of Christ worldwide.

Future

LEANING FORWARD: MOVEMENT IDENTITY AND MISSION

The Church of God movement has used the phrase "Church of God" less as a formal group name and more to emphasize the fact that the Body of God's people belong to God and to none other. God calls into being, gifts, governs, and sends the church on mission into the world as a Divine and not a human body.

The 1995 biography of this movement's primary pioneer, Daniel S. Warner, is properly titled *It's God's Church!* Given this primary truth, how does a particular body of believers understand its own distinctive identity and role within the larger body of the church? Answering this question is an important goal of today's Church of God movement.

31

IDENTITY AND MISSION OF THE MOVEMENT

The General Assembly and its corporate body, Church of God Ministries, are not intended to be "ecclesiastical" in the sense of officially framing required beliefs and structures for the lives of the congregations of the Church of God movement. Nonetheless, they are the most prominent corporate voices of this movement as a whole, and they regularly seek ways to stimulate and communicate the best thinking of the movement's leaders.

Two major gatherings of Church of God leaders, recently convened under the auspices of the General Assembly, have concluded that there is urgent need for the Church of God movement today to have a fresh understanding of its identity and mission. According to the Strategic Planning Conference of 2006, "we need to determine the core of our mission and then engineer a new Movement DNA that focuses on that mission."

The Roundtable of "Project Imagine" in 2017-2018 frequently voiced the following assumption. "While some structural change is clearly needed, no structural change can be the full solution to the present challenges. Beneath the obvious structural concerns lies the core need of clarifying the movement's *present identity and mission*. A clear 'why' enables a workable 'how.' Such missional understanding of the movement has eroded in recent decades and must be reclaimed."

Precedent

In its earliest literature, the identity of the Church of God movement was often identified in negative terms. There were things that it intentionally wanted *not to be*. The early movement denounced certain failures of the institutional church of the time. By contrast, its own identity and mission were to involve a deliberate "coming out" of such failures and a returning to the authority of the Bible and its revealed pattern of God's intended church.

There was to be no more human "denominationalizing" of God's church, but instead a "movement" of God's Spirit that enables a holy people who are united together for accomplishing God's mission in this world. Thus, "non-denominational" and "non-sectarian" were common identifications of the early Church of God movement.

Daniel S. Warner (1842-1895) was the primary pioneer of the Church of God movement. Rather than claiming novel truths, he understood himself to be a re-discoverer, re-affirmer, and re-experiencer of what had been basic to biblical Christianity from its beginning. His intent was that there not be just another church among the churches, but a movement among the churches on behalf of the well-being of the church as a whole.

The masthead of the movement's early periodical, the *Gospel Trumpet*, read: "Definite, Radical, and Anti-Sectarian, Sent Forth in the Name of the Lord Jesus Christ, for the Publication of Full Salvation, Healing of the Body, and the Unity of All True Christians in 'the Faith Once Delivered to the Saints.'"

Future threads

Much has changed since the 1880s, both in society at large and in the life of God's people. Altered cultural and church patterns of believing and relating have brought the necessity of reassessment of how holiness and unity, central theological concerns of the Church of God movement, are to be defined and implemented.

One way a "movement" remains faithful to its original vision is to remain dynamic and flexible, continuing to move toward the will of God for each new time. The self-understanding of the Church of God movement has eroded over time. There has been delay in adjusting to change with fresh self-understanding. The movement has matured from clusters of isolated individuals in the Mid-Western United States to a very large number of congregations scattered around the globe.

How should this current body of believers understand itself and its contemporary mission? As chapter thirty makes clear, the understanding must be formulated in part by and relevant to today's global movement. The General Assembly in the United States and Canada hopes to enable today's world-wide movement to "lean forward" into this critical task of freshly understanding itself under God. Pioneers of the Church of God movement should be respected without being mirrored uncritically in this very new time.

The goal of this church body's future self-understanding hardly centers in the formulation of a formal and mandatory creed, although engaging together in serious theological exploration is very important. See chapter thirty for a brief record of past conferences, dialogues, and consultations that have pioneered this task. Rather than a formal creed, the Church of God movement has affirmed basic elements of belief and particular theological perspectives thought crucial for the whole Body of Christ. These inform ongoing identity.

Three foundational elements of belief have been judged above question (see chapter twenty-one). These theological basics enable the people of God to have biblical integrity. At least seven particular theological perspectives also have been affirmed by the Church of God movement and held on behalf of the fuller health and mission effectiveness of the whole church (see chapter thirty). These perspectives enable the people of God to be united and equipped to serve today's world in the name and Spirit of Christ.

These three basic belief elements, then, when joined with these seven particular perspectives, combine to frame the core of the historic and future identity and mission of this Church of God movement among God's people and on behalf of a lost world. One simple presentation of this identity and mission was captured in the "ARISE!" theme of the 2006 Strategic Planning Conference of the Church of God:

> **A**nnounce God's good news to the world;
>
> **R**elate as God's Spirit-born children;
>
> **I**nvest for the sake of God's kingdom;
>
> **S**hare in response to God's call; and
>
> **E**mpower God's gifted people for ministry.

32

PRIORITY ARENAS AND FOUNDATIONS OF FUTURE MINISTRY

The General Director of Church of God Ministries, James Lyon, was ratified by the 2019 General Assembly for a second six-year term of office. In addressing the Assembly, he identified six arenas of priority future ministry to be developed and implemented through Church of God Ministries with his enthusiastic support. They are:

Leadership Focus—preparing future ministerial leadership;

CARE—investing in ministerial financial well-being;

Pacific Coast Collective—pioneering a model of efficient assembly cooperation;

The Global Church of God—seeking a venue for coordinated international strategic planning and cooperative ministry.

As foundation for these and all other potential program thrusts, Lyon also stated again five proposed *theological non-negotiables*. As part of the 2013 process of being interviewed for the key leadership role of General Director of Church of God Ministries, James Lyon had asked all present to write down the five theological non-negotiables of the Church of God movement as each understood them. "I wanted to test the waters and see what kind of theological drama, if any, might unfold if I left my pastorate and moved into this new arena."

Lyon was astonished at the outcome, deeply affected by the unity that surfaced among "these forty of the church's brightest and best." These five theological non-negotiables do not represent any authoritative voice for the Church of God movement beyond Director Lyon's. Even so, they are clearly his and widely embraced by many others. In fact, on the 2019 occasion of his ratification for a second term as General Director, he repeated with passion to the General Assembly these non-negotiables. They again were well received. They are:

First: **Jesus is Lord.** The singularity, exclusivity, and divinity of the one Lord Jesus stand tall. The Bread of Life. The Water of Life. The Lamb of God. The Way, the Truth, and the Life. The one Mediator between God and humankind. The Lord of lords, the King of kings. The Son of Man. The Son of God. The Word become flesh. The Name at which every knee shall bow. *Jesus is the subject.* This defines us.

Second: **Holiness.** The Person, work, and power of the Holy Spirit are fundamental to who we are as a people. We unabashedly own the truth that the Spirit can transform us, possess us, equip us, and empower us. It is the work of the Holy Spirit that sanctifies us, makes us holy, sets us apart for sacred service, and seals us for eternity's sake. It is the Spirit who convicts us of sin and enables us to overcome sin. It is the Holy Spirit who can breathe supernatural gifts into us, for Jesus' sake. He is the Comforter promised by Jesus and the witness of our redemption. This defines us.

Third: **Unity.** We are a people uniquely called by God to be a catalyst for Christian unity, believing that the division of the body of Christ is hell's greatest weapon to thwart heaven's ends in this world. We are convinced that the splintering of the body is not the Lord's work, but the enemy's. We believe that hell trembles at the prospect of a people united, redeemed by the blood, possessed by the Spirit. Unity is not for us an also-ran on the to-do list of God, but a primary driver of who and why we are called out. It defines us.

Fourth: **The Great Commandments.** Love God with your whole self, and love your neighbors as yourself. The Scripture tells us this is the sum of the Law and the Prophets. When a teacher of the Law sought to test Jesus (Luke 10), asking, "What must I do to have eternal life?" Jesus asked him what he read in the Scripture. When the man replied with the Great Commandments, Jesus approved, saying, "You have answered well; do this and you will live." As a people in the pursuit of holiness, the Great Commandments clothe us. They define us.

And, fifth: **The Supremacy of Scripture.** We are a people of the Book, the Good Book, the Holy Bible, the Old and New Testaments, supernaturally inspired, preserved across time, cultures, and continents, delivered to us, useful for reproof and instruction in righteousness. The Scripture is our ultimate field of inquiry and judgment, the measure of conduct, faith, and practice. Whatever the question, whatever the test, whatever comes before us, in the end, it is the Scripture, above all other disciplines, that informs and defines us. This is a non-negotiable. It is who we are.

The Church of God movement, rooted in these core beliefs and global perspectives, now faces today's challenge to arise, keep moving, keep believing, keep reaching, stay relevant, always determined to actively *lean forward!* as God may direct.

INDEX

SUBJECTS AND PERSONS

www.ingramcontent.com/pod-product-compliance
Lightning Source LLC
Chambersburg PA
CBHW051838090426
42736CB00011B/1863